Ashli D. Wells
Cartoon Sculptor/Poet

Ashli D. Wells
Cartoon Sculptor/Poet

words and pictures by Ashli D. Wells

Ashli D. Wells: Cartoon Sculptor/Poet

Copyright © Ashli D. Wells

All rights reserved. No part of this book may be used or reproduced by any means, graphic, electronic, or mechanical, including photocopying, recording, taping or by any information storage retrieval system without the written permission of the publisher except in the case of brief quotations embodied in critical articles and reviews.

This book and my life are dedicated to God, Po, Thud, Elmo.
Happy 52nd birthday to me. This book is my birthday present to me.
I feel very blessed to be an old lady… sure beats the alternative.

I'm on the road to rich and famous, stuck in the town of poor and unknown.

Dreams
A Fool's Creed

They advised me not to do it, for
they said it just could not be done.
To even try is simply impossible but I did it, and it was fun.
Yes, those who know how to dream can accomplish
impossible things.
When the odds are at their worst, remember that
someone has to be first.
That someone could very well be you, if
you don't listen to what you can't do.

My name is Ashli D. Wells. I'm an artist based in Fort Worth, Texas. I sculpt people and animals in cartoon form. These days I mostly sculpt dogs because dogs are awesome, fun creatures that make folks happy. With everything that occurs in the world, I try to create happy whenever I can. I know some folks may have their doubts about a gal who sits around and mostly sculpts cartoon dogs all the time but I promise that

it is a real job.

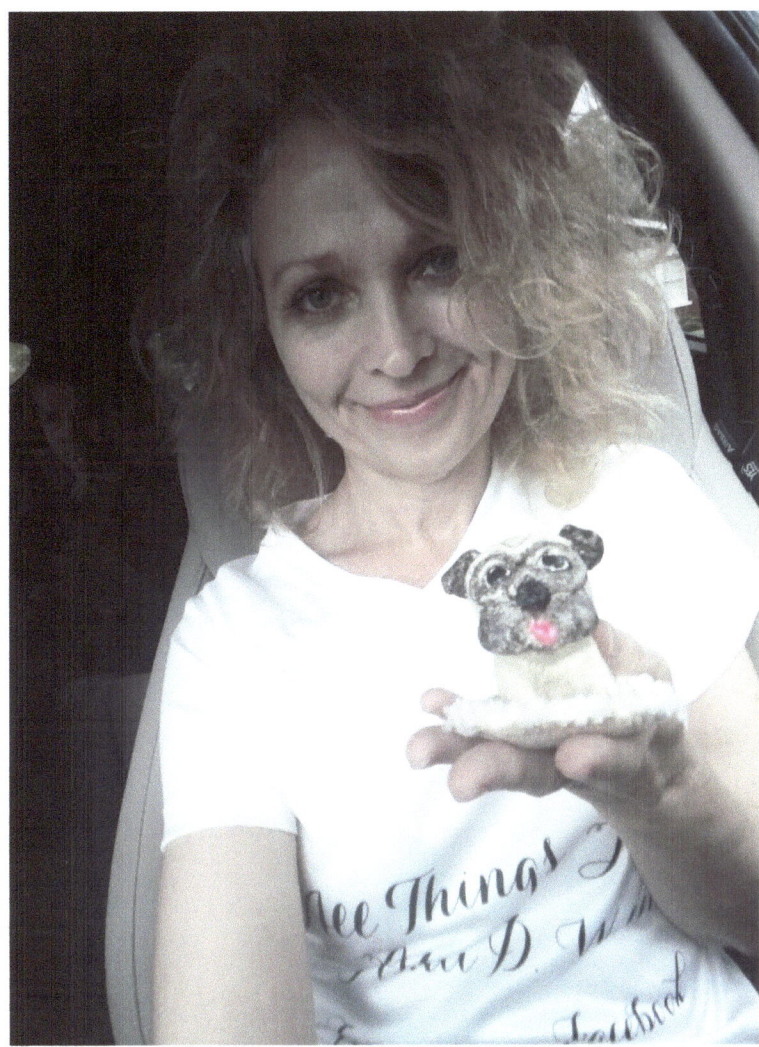

I love what I do. I take real people and animals and create their alter egos in cartoon form in polymer clay. My job is really fun. Turn the page to find out my secret to do what I do.

My secret is that I have kept at least part of my brain stuck at four- years- old, and try to view life thru that lens. I try to see the good and the happy in everything and everyone. I get super excited, probably too excited, about eating ice cream sandwiches, spending a day in my jammies, watching cartoons, playing with puppies and kittens, and running from point A to point B like a little kid. I love puddles of everything but pee (since I am a grownup those don't bring me joy after I got old enough to be responsible for cleaning them up.) I love all other puddles that a person can splash in.

Little

I used to be little.
I used to be loud.
I used to lay in the grass staring at clouds.

I used to be messy.
I wouldn't walk, I'd run.
I used to think life was so much more fun.

I'd talk and not listen.
I colored outside the lines.
I'd step in puddles and be just fine.

Now I no longer fidget or wiggle around.
I can sit quietly, and not make a sound.

But I used to laugh louder.
I'd jump up and down
back when my life was more smiles than frowns.

Vrrooom

I've got this little boy who is a whole lot like his dad.

He likes big trucks with big wheels.

Such excitement he feels,

and he wants one real real bad.

The bigger the truck the better.

Loud motors make him cheer.

The best part of his day

is when he smiles and can say,

"Mom, the school bus is HERE!"

Penny in my Pocket

I have a penny in my pocket,
a pebble in my shoe.
a booger in my nose,
my tongue has turned blue.
My hair is standing up.
My hands have turned black.
Something red is on my shirt
as if I've been attacked.
My shoes are all untied.
It's a wonder I'm alive.
But I run across the playground,
grinning ear to ear.
I look so very happy without a tinge of fear.
What happened to me today?
Why am I such a mess?
Well, today simply was one of the very best.
I found a penny in the dirt.
Digging made my hands turn black.
The red on my shirt it ketchup,
leftover from my snack.
My hair is on end because it was windy outside.
I ran so very fast that my shoes came all untied.
This pebble came aboard when I slid down from the hill.
My tongue is blue from candy…it's really no big deal.
The booger in my nose, well it's barely there.
You have a big one too, so why is it that you care?

Trouble

I hate timeout. I really do. I do not think it's fair.
I try to voice my opinion but no one seems to care.
What is my crime for this hard time? Whatever did I do?
Did I speak out of turn, get too loud, or did I spill my glue?
I promise it wasn't me that did what you think was done.
Your getting mad only serves to make this more un-fun.
Once again, I'm condemned, wrongly accused and tried.
You can take away my recess but I still have my pride.

However, I am not a total ditz that lives in some unrealistic utopia in my head. It is just that everyone has one thing or another to deal with. There are going to be times when life is more something that a person struggles to get through, as opposed to something that is actually fun. Sometimes I was not the one in the fire but I was just close enough in to feel the burn.

Hard Knocks

I've got 32 cents and God between the rest of the world and me.
My job isn't great. My bills are all late. I'm not sure what I want to be.
It isn't just me that is stuck in this rut that gets deeper all the time.
Everything around me is such a mess that no one seems to be fine.
I don't know how to fix it. I don't know what to do.
It is all so overwhelming that actually I should be through.
I should have thrown in the towel long ago on a life that seems all wrong.
I should have left behind these people, this place, for I just don't belong.
But somehow, I made it through. Somehow, I am still here.
Somehow my days are mostly good, and I don't live in fear.
Somehow my kids are happy. Somehow my life has love.
Since the 32 cents can't do that then it must be the man above.

Regret

We would change it if we could.
We would turn all the bad to good.
We would go back and say the words we left unspoken.
We would right all of our wrongs.
We would've made you feel like you belong.
We would've done our best to keep your heart from feeling broken.
We would have done so much but we didn't,
and such now we are left with so much sorrow.
For all we didn't do, we would have done if we knew
we could have had a different tomorrow.
We thought but didn't do it.
We had our chance….we blew it.

Distance

I just want to touch you
to feel your breath on my skin
to wrap my arms around you
to let you come within
within my secret world
where only you can dwell
to make me come alive
to make heaven from my hell
to put a twinkle in my eye
and a smile on my face
all the worries of this world
you so easily erase
I want you close enough to whisper
I need to tell you dear
how much I truly love you
how much I need you here

My Knight

You had better pray that I never remember.
You can bet that I will never forget.
A whole lot of stuff seemed to go down, the last time that we met.
I had a really bad day and was searching for a friend.
High on that white horse, you came riding in.
A true hero, or at least for the world to see.
Too bad, all of that seemed to wear off when you got with me.
Things started out well, just talking about family and stuff.
That part I remember but that's when things get tough.
I'm not quite sure what transpired that got us from point A to B.
It is all fragmented, hazy, and a little unreal that the girl was even me.
Something must have happened within a very short time span.
Was it something spur of the moment or did you have a plan?
All I know is that as friends we were not that tight.
What went down on that night is so far off from right.
I remember just enough and it replays in my mind.
Seems to me that you went a little beyond trying to be kind.
I cried for a few days as things I began to recall.
I hope it was good for you and that you had a ball.
I bet you thought I would hide away. silent in my own private hell.
I guess you really did not know this girl all that well.
After the sadness faded away then I started to get mad.
I realized that horse was gray not white, and the good guy was really bad.
I opted out of hiding out and feeling like I wanted to die.
I looked at the good things in my life and my tears began to dry.
I came out of my house and stepped back into the world.
Not the same fragile being, I was a brand new girl.
The fun is over for you now, think of what you stand to lose.
To never venture back in my world is what you should wisely choose.
You messed me up a little and gave me a small slice of hell.
Good thing this gal has God and a C.H.L.

The Plan

Sometimes when a baby is born, things don't turn out as planned.

They may look a little different, or even

fit in the palm of your hand.

But if that time should come, hold faith and don't let go

'cause God knows what He is doing, and He will let it show.

Sometimes our little bundles of joy come into this world just great

then something happens later on and parents have to wait:

for important news, still holding on, and praying for the best.

Sometimes that is what we get, and then we get a little rest.

Sooner or later, along the line, yes something comes along

and when it comes to children and God's love,

He is always holding on.

For that plan is out there. You just didn't make it,

and should someday something happen, God will help you take it.

The Village

There was a cat who sat on a log who talked to a bird who sang to a frog

who played with a mouse who ran from a squirrel who had a bug on his head

and this is their world.

The cat was fat for all day he did lay stretched out on a log each sunny day

while chatting away with the bird overhead who sang out loudly from his cozy nest bed.

The frog hipped and hopped below with his little mouse friend as together they danced until the bird's songs would end,

or until the mouse could no longer stay for the he would see the much larger squirrel running his way.

The little mouse would run so far and so fast that his frog friend finally felt the need to ask,

"Mr. Squirrel, Why do you chase my mouse friend so? For now we can't dance since he had to go."

The squirrel answered," Whatever do you mean? Let me explain, for things are not as they seem.

I have a bug on my head who told me to run. I am not chasing mouse. We are just having fun.

So the bug holds tight while I run fast. For as long as I run, his joy will last.

So blame it on the bug who likes a wild ride. It is not my fault your mouse friend should hide.

Your mouse friend can come out from where he has hidden, and if he wants, have his turn, after my bug friend has ridden."

So the little mouse tiptoed out from behind a tree, and since he was not dinner, decided friends they would be.

So now the cat sits on a log and talks to the bird who sings to a frog in a happier world

where a squirrel and a mouse and bug together enjoy life's wild ride,

and not one of them runs and no one does hide, for they learned not to judge by what they thought they did see .

They took time to ask questions and the truth set them free.

So if a cat, a bird, a frog, a mouse, a squirrel and a bug can learn not to worry,

then maybe the rest of the word should not be in such a hurry.

We should also take the time to understand what we see

because what we see might not be at all what actually might be.

Doctor's Time

So you went to the doctor and now you think you are going to die.

But you ain't dead yet, so get back up. Let me tell you why.

I know you think that doctor is really, really bright

but what are you going to do if that guy ain't really, really right?

I guess you could just lay down, and I'll go call the hearse.

But I still need you around, so please listen to my verse.

No, I'm not some big doctor, and I'm not even very smart.

But if you check out at this time, you are going to take my heart.

I need my heart. It keeps me alive, and I'm not through living.

Some folks seem to think they still need you around,

and you've got a lot of giving.

So if you are dead set on going, I guess I'll help you pack

but realize you will leave a lot behind.

You ain't coming back.

I guess you could change your mind, and decide that you are

going to live a little longer.

Who knows, even when you go, our hearts may get a little stronger.

What I'm trying to say is simple. I knew you were going to die.

I didn't have to go to medical school to learn the reason why.

It happens to everyone, sooner or later, when it is his time;

but if you were smart, you'd save my heart and not step right in line.

'Cause doctor's time is just not right. They are always running late.

So if you plan to up and die, it's probably okay to wait.

Parents

I wish that my parents could come to
school and speak on career day
but one is in jail, the other on drugs,
so who knows what they would say.
Oh, I'm okay. My needs are met but
not by the way they are living.
Grandpa and Grandma take care of me
and provide all that I'm given.
Yes, Mom and Dad do as they please and
show up every once in awhile.
They tell me jokes, and excuses, but mostly
excuses, and they expect to make me smile.
As I have gotten older and I understand
more, I figured it out on my own.
My mom and dad may have made me but
they never made me a home.
Mom and Dad took care of their needs and
because of the decisions they made,
they may have made me but they failed me as
parents, and that is the price that I paid.

Rehab

Some people want to go to far away places.

Some just want to go to the mall.

Me, I dream of the day that I can get up and just walk down the hall.

I just want to go to the bathroom, and I want to go all by myself.

I want to bathe and dress, and get around without anyone else's help.

I want to wiggle my fingers and toes and

be able to scratch my own nose.

I want to get up and go to eat whenever and whatever that I choose.

I want to put on and tie my own tennis shoes.

I know that day will come but it won't be tomorrow.

I guess there is no sense in laying here in a bed full of sorrow.

I'll be proud of what I can do today. Maybe the

next day, I'll try to do a little more.

My fate is not sealed by far. Only God knows what is in store.

Though I can't walk today, someday I might run a mile.

So with that thought in mind, I will lay in this bed and smile.

Empty

When you died you left an empty spot that no one can ever fill.

You took a piece of my heart, a chunk of my

soul and a whole lot of my will

to just go on, day to day, and try not to be so sad.

Without a doubt, the day that you left was the worst I've ever had.

I will never forget that day. I relive it so much.

The hurt is so overwhelmingly strong.

The pain is so fresh. The wound still unhealed,

though it has been so very long.

I've always been told that time heals all hurt

but I'm still waiting to get to that day.

But when the loss is so great, the pain more

intense, it never seems to go away.

Some days are tougher than others, imagining

life with you still here with me.

It's hard to want something so badly that

you know can just never be.

I'm surrounded by reminders of your life

and all the love you gave me.

It's those sweet memories of you here,

which I hold dear that sometimes have to save me.   .

Mommy Don't Cry

I've going to get well.

I'm going to be fine.

Just you wait and see.

All the doctors and nurses will do their jobs

and take good care of me.

I know that it hurts, and that it's hard;

but someday this will be done.

We will go home to our house, get some

rest and get back to having fun.

Don't worry. I'll be okay.

I promise not to die.

Just trust in God to see us through, and Mommy, please don't cry.

Miss It

Is it really funny? Are you really being cool,

when you tease and tear apart the other kids in school.

I know that you may be popular and have a lot of friends,

but do not be surprised to learn that those friendships often end.

Also, sooner or later, one of them will find something wrong with you.

When you become the topic of jokes, whatever will you do?

Life is no beauty contest or a race to have the best car.

It does not matter where you buy your clothes or who the makers are.

What counts most is what is inside that makes each child his own,

not who his parents are, or how large is their home.

So if you are the kid who gets pleasure from other's pain,

be aware that all parents quickly learn your name.

If you want to be known for something

try getting a reputation for being nice.

Being cruel is nothing more than a really ugly vice.

Besides, things are going to change a lot when you are grown.

If being mean was your way, you will find out that YOU were wrong.

The least attractive child in your class may grow up to look better than all the rest.

The poorest kid in town my become the millionaire with all the best.

The little chubby kid may lose all of that weight.

The child that never said a word may grow up to say things great.

You cannot go back when you are grown and redo what you have wronged.

You cannot make the child you teased feel like he belonged.

Remember the Golden Rule and practice it at school.

You will find that being nice is so extremely cool.

However, if being mean is the role that you want to fit,

know that every hurtful remark could go away,

and no one would even miss it!

Differences

I'm not gay, I'm straight

but that gives me no reason to hate.

I'm not black. I'm white

but that doesn't make me wrong or right.

My God and yours don't share the same name

but I can try to understand you just the same.

Though our differences are way too many to name,

if we learn to accept and respect then we become the same:

individuals with fears, desires, needs, and love

getting by with a lot of help from above.

If we could just get along,

our world would be a happier home.

If you only like those like you,

you will wind up sad and alone.

I have two poems called Gone which I know is confusing but it fits both of them.

Gone

I can't see who you used to be.

I can't love a man who isn't there.

I can't pray and hope and keep

any longer: it's simply just not fair.

The man I loved is long gone.

His memory faded away.

A stranger took his place

and I can't let him stay.

I'm so tired of how things are.

I never thought we'd wind up like this.

Go on. Close down the bar.

There's nothing home left to miss.

Blame work. Blame God. Blame me.

Drown in that bottle alone.

Through bloodshot eyes you'll see: I'm already gone.

Gone

It hit me this morning that you were gone.
There is no sound of your voice.
You won't ring my phone.
I won't see you later.
You won't walk through that door.
For the rest of my life,
of you , there's no more.
It's strange here without you.
with pieces still there:
your things, your shoes, the clothes that you wear.
My daily routine is all out of whack.
I just sit here alone and pray you come back.
I'm not quite sure what I should do.
I had no vision of me without you.
You are still alive and well here in my mind,
as real as the stuff that you left behind.

Wait for Me

Save me a spot when you get there.

I will be coming a little later on.

This place won't be the same without you.

This world won't feel much like my home.

I hope that when you get to Heaven that you have really good ears.

Because I'll still need to talk to you, and I'll be stuck down here.

My Child

I know that you are hurt, that you are sick,

and that your life is fading fast.

As hard as it is to see you like this, if only this moment could last.

I brought you into this world never wanting to see you leave.

It should not be you at this moment in time,

oh how I prayed for it to be me.

The love this parent has for you, child, is like no earthly other.

As much as I love you, as much joy as we have had,

right now, I don't want to be your mother.

I want to be you, to take your place, and

to go to your Heavenly home.

It would feel more just, more right with less

pain if I were the one to be gone.

I'm not alone in my feelings for you, your dad feels the very same.

As hard as it is to let you go, we know your

soul has been saved in Jesus's name.

The Answer

What if I'm not that smart?

What if I'm kind of poor?

What if someday my legs won't carry me through the door?

Will those around try to help me, or will they pass me by?

I wish I knew the answer; or if not, at least the reason why.

When I Grow Up

When I grow up, no one will hit me or touch me in a bad way.

When I grow up, I will have plenty of food

and people will care what I say.

When I grow up, I will have people who

love, and help take care of me.

When I grow up, no one will tell me that

I'm stupid and all the things that I can't be.

I wish that I didn't have to wait 'til I'm

grown for it seems so far away.

I'm just a small child alone in this world,

so for these things each night I pray.

What were you thinking?

It may be your spouse, your best friend, your boss or significant other,

your neighbor, your leader, your child, or even be your mother.

Sometimes you honestly can't tell if they are kidding, crazy, or drinking.

It fits with many answers and is the question that you are often thinking.

It defies any and all explanations, applies to all people and nations.

The question most asked, on misguided paths, is "What were you thinking?"

Why did you open your mouth and say what you already said?

It is way too late now but I bet you wish you were dead.

Why did you go and do that? Do you have no thought process at all?

And since you mind was set, why didn't you think to call?

Why did you buy that thing that needs a little fixing?

Why did you even go out and do a little mixing?

Who picked your date? How could you be late or show up the way that you are?

Who did your hair? What did you wear? Why did you buy that car?

Why did you teach your kids to talk if you only knew what they would be saying?

Would you have even let them go out, if you had known what they'd be playing?

Why did you commit to that; or align yourself in that way?

Are you on drugs, or are you in love? Why is it that you stay?

Why did you tell your friends that:

'cause you thought they wouldn't tell.

Had you not heard that before, been there again, and didn't it feel like hell.

There are times when actions, reactions, and motives defy all logic and reason.

Those are usually some of our most memorable times, though often not quite pleasing.

We've all been there before, will go there again, yet no one has the directions.

It's done. It's over. It's said, and it's too late for corrections.

However, when you wind up there, remember that you are not alone.

Some people go there so much that it's almost like a second home.

Even if there is no great tragedy, ordinary stuff happens, and we all suffer from that damage.

Home Improvement

I asked my spouse to fix the roof, now we have buckets in the attic.

The kitchen sink sprung a leak.

He said, "Don't worry, I'll attack it."

Now when I am getting thirsty and wanting water to drink,

I must head down the hall to the bathroom:

the only place left with a sink.

I thought I wanted to paint the bedroom,

and he insisted on helping with that.

He did a good job on the walls;

now my dresser is Interior Eggshell Flat.

He offered to replace the kitchen cabinets but

I said,"Honey,Why? What For?"

I knew I'd be left with my pans

in boxes strewn all over the floor.

I wonder what I was thinking now that our money is all but spent.

I pray my kids don't get cold outside in their little backyard tent.

I love my husband but can't take more of his home improvement.

I wish I had asked at the start of the tasks if he knew how to do it.

Kids

I've read all the books, watched all the shows,

garnered advice from the best of my friends.

Nothing works. It's no good or no use.

I still have no means to the ends.

They won't eat, won't sleep, won't do what they're told,

and can't seem at all to be good.

Whatever I did, whatever I've tried,

it didn't work like the books said it should.

So I have no recourse, no other plan,

I've exhausted all reason and rhyme.

What I do next might not be the best

but it has been proven with time.

Yes, I'm avoiding the advice of all the best sources

with the best plans of what to do next.

Whatever it takes to make these kids mind

is not written in the words of a text.

I have one last resort, one final chance to save myself from this zoo.

I'll pick up the phone and make that call to find out what Nana would do.

Homebound

Everything I own is broken or sticky.

Everything I pay is a little bit late.

The rear seat of my car is a little bit icky.

I can't remember when I had my last date.

I don't go on exotic vacations to discover what other cultures do.

However I have traveled and searched all over

for the missing sock, book and shoe.

My job skills may be fading, and I don't

really remember what I did.

My life changed so drastically after the birth of my kids.

Nothing is the tidy little package that it used to be.

I'm overworked, underpaid, and I don't have a minute that's free.

I spend my days picking boogers, cleaning barf,

and keeping little ones occupied.

My patience sometimes leaves me, and my nerves are often fried.

I could go back to work and leave all this madness behind.

They could go to daycare all day, and no one much would mind.

However after living this life for so very long,

spending my days any other way would feel extremely wrong.

I like being the one who can always make things right.

I love being the one who can always end the fight.

I would miss being there for all the little victories.

I look forward to being there for all their coming history.

Leaving this behind, at this point, is just something that I can't do.

So I'll keep being a stay-at-home mom and searching for that lost shoe.

Coworker

Side by side here we go, another day on the job.

I know your talk, your walk, your kids,

and your kitty cat named Bob,

I know what ails you, fails you, and worse what brings you joy.

I'm stuck and I'm here

till that transfer does clear.

Only then will you cease to annoy.

The Drive-thru

I cannot understand you.

DO I NEED TO YELL?

I want a burger, big fries and a cola of whatever kind you sell.

Well, I'm finally at the window.

This is just not right at all.

It's a chicken and an apple pie,

and the fries are really small.

I hate to be a pain but I don't think this is mine.

What's that you say?

It's free: NO WAY —

In that case, then it's fine.

grown

I want a do-over, a chance to start brand new.

I need to turn the clock way back to spend more time with you.

I'd be fine with day one, or the day that I brought you home.

Standing here before me, I can't believe you're grown.

Where did all the years go, and why did they go so fast?

How can it be that your childhood days are all part of our past?

I have boxes and boxes of pictures drawn by hands so very little.

I have photos, trophies, and ribbons from all the years in the middle.

I remember when you learned to drive,

your first job, and your first date.

I remember how scared I was that time when you came home late.

We have been through so much together and share so very much love.

Before you head out to conquer the world, I'm here to collect my hug.

No matter where this life takes you, or if things sometimes get crazy,

I'm still here for you, from here on out,

'cause you'll always be my baby

The End

Sometimes it's not forever.

Sometimes it's no longer fun.

Sometimes despite the best of attempts,

it all just comes undone.

Sometimes it's all your fault.

Sometimes you're not to blame.

Sometimes without reason,

things just aren't the same.

Lives can be wasted on whatever went wrong.

Living requires letting go and learning to move on.

However, I got thru things, sorted it all out, and decided what is important and what defines me. I never want to be known for the bad things that have happened to me. I want to have my identity based on the things that I have worked for that are good, and totally forget the bad.

Real

You might not agree with all that I do.
You might not like everything that I say.
However, my goal is to be true to myself,
so I just can't be any other way.
Accept me if you will.
To hate me is your right.
I don't expect an easy ride, and I won't run from a fight.
You may find me quite lovable, and we always agree.
In truth, I find the latter doubtful if I am being me.
With all said, to get along, whatever must we do?
I think to start it would be good if you could just be you.

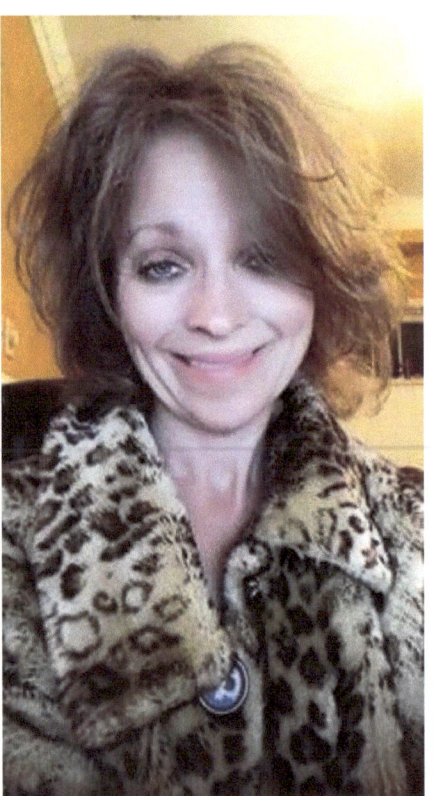

Totally sober pic of me after an all-nighter doing polymer clay.

Surprisingly, I found this awesome coat at a thrift store. I bet no one saw that coming.

Our Blessed Home

We don't need granite counter tops, brass faucets, or a Jacuzzi tub.

We are happy as we can be in our little house filled with love.

Though small by some standards is the place that we call home;

we would feel as blessed as the richest of men

surrounded by our love alone.

Many a man has lived a sad life in a mansion high on a hill,

blind to the fact that the wealth of a home

is the way that it makes you feel.

My Son

You look just like your daddy.

You act just like him, too.

You like outside, and sometimes hide

from what Mama wants you to do.

Somewhere along the line,

you learned how to get out of trouble.

You look at me and smile that smile,

and I swear I'm seeing double.

Shine

If I could be a star, I'd shine my light on you.

When the night got dark and scary, I would shine on through.

I'd hang out in the heavens so very high above you.

I'd shine bright in the darkest of nights to show how much I love you.

If you got lost along the way, you could count on me to be there.

My light would pierce the darkest times to show how much I do care.

I'd lead you along the way till you arrived safely home.

I'd hover over always so that you'd never feel alone.

Wherever night may find you, just take a look above.

Let the diamonds in the sky remind you of our precious love.

The Worm

There was a little worm who went about his way so slow.
Whenever he might arrive, his friends would never know.
But along the way, he took in all the sights.
He stopped to smell the flowers.
He paused on starry nights.
He enjoyed the beauty of all there was around.
Thus ,the slow little worm never seemed to frown.

Priceless

The finest of the gifts that a mother loves

are slobbery little kisses and sticky little hugs.

I know

In my darkest hours,

when all hope I've lost,

during helpless desperation,

I may feel all chances are shot.

When faith in myself is gone,

and I don't know what to do,

when I'm all cried out and exhausted,

I can always count on you.

I will not always have the answers

or always do the right things;

but if I learn to trust in you,

I will have the gifts that this devotion brings.

Peace, love and strength, no matter how hard the task

are always mine for the taking

if I only remember to ask.

You are always with me no matter what I do.

Dear God in Heaven when I am lost,

I find everything that I need in you.

My Friend

You are my friend until the end.

When you hurt, I feel your pain.

Whether dazed or confused or upset with bad news,

you offer comfort without looking for blame.

In the midst of this insanity caused by this species of

humanity, things don't always go our way.

We got ourselves where we are,

yet we avoid that by far;

and we pray daily for change.

Through life we will go, uphill mostly though,

and I have no clue where this thing ends.

But one thing is for sure, there's not a pill or a cure

that is stronger than one real, true friend.

Simple ME

My life is better than it has ever been.

I'm at a place where I want to be.

I'm not counted among great and powerful men,

but I am happy being simply me.

Funny

My mom works as a clown, seriously,

which I do not think is funny at all.

She has a red nose, and shoes with long toes,

and a car that is the tiniest of small.

She has wigs of all colors with bloomers to match,

and a horn that honks really loud.

It is hard to be cool when your chauffeur to school

always draws such a crowd.

She does not get that she totally stands out.

The other kids won't leave me alone.

I would complain but it would be in vain,

for she is way more unusual at home.

Face Value

What if I had a big wart on my nose and an extra ear?

Would you cuddle me, kiss me, and pull me close,

or would you run in fear?

What if my skin turned green, and I lost all of my hair?

Would you long to be near me always,

or would I give you quite a scare?

What if I was really tall and reached all the way up to the sky?

Would I still be your best bud, or would I make you cry?

I want to know for sure that you love what makes me — ME —

and not just love what is on the outside that you obviously see.

Please answer these questions truthfully.

My heart is hanging on the line.

Will you be here forever and always, and we be truly fine?

Well, here are my answers to hopefully put your heart at ease.

I trust that time will show your heart that I only aim to please.

If you had a big wart on your nose,

I could find you easily in a crowd.

With that extra ear, I wouldn't have to shout,

"I love you" quite so loud.

Green skin would come in handy on Halloween.

Not having any hair just makes you easier to clean.

If you were tall as a giant and hit your head on a cloud,

to be someone loved by you would still make me extremely proud.

After I summed up all the damage and wear and tear of life, I chose(that is a decision) to like myself, and luckily some other folks decided that they liked me like I really was, too. I also made a conscious choice to forgive myself for the bazillion things that I have done wrong in life and let go of that baggage, and also let go of anyone that could not do the same.

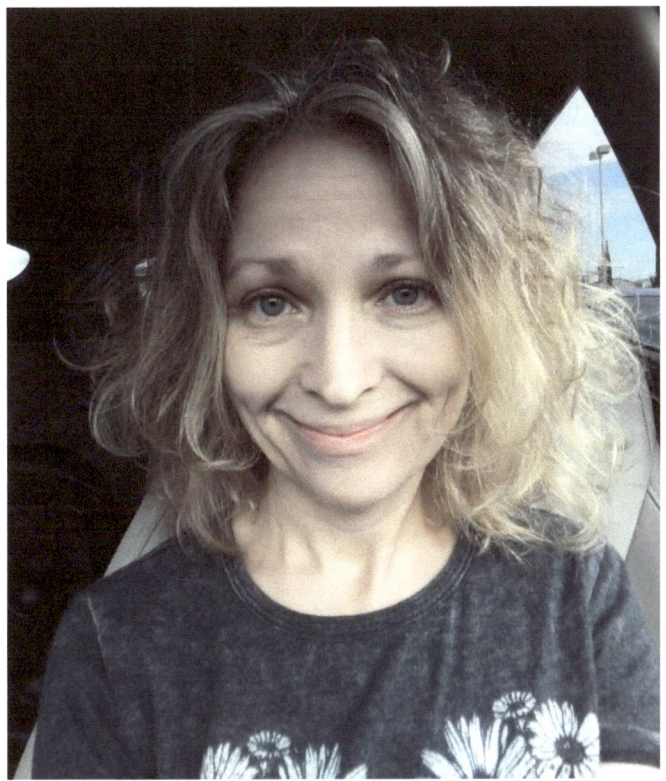

Mercy

You did not ruin my life, for I am still breathing yet.
I could hold on to hatred but I choose to forgive and forget.
So when I pray for God's healing power to help get me through,
I pray not just for myself….I also pray for you.

Pause

If you knew what lay ahead, would you even go?
If given the choice to wonder, would you rather know?
Looking back behind us, we all have twists and turns.
Would you risk it all for what the heart still yearns?
There is only so much precious time in this life we live.
To satisfy your heart, how much would you give?

I just decided to not be defined by the bad. The bad will always be there but I choose to see the good, and make the happy memories the ones that I save. I try to learn from the bad experiences to help make me into a better person. I hold onto the good and look to the future with hope. I focus on preserving the happy. It is not any fun continually reliving the sad drama and trauma of life. I'm not talking about tuning everything out or being disrespectful or apathetic to what goes on in the world around a person. I am just referring to not being consumed by our own tragedies to the point that we cease to function as healthy individuals. I think most folks work too hard at what they do that is good to be totally defined by some random act of tragedy. I know that I feel no need to discuss or relive my personal pain when I can opt to rather use that time and energy to make a little dose of happy. Somethings are harder than others to get over, and I do think a person gains strength to a certain extent from reminiscing over prior hardships because that can create somewhat of a mentality of look what I have overcome…but there comes a point when too much is just too much and in creeps dysfunction. Anyway, I had to let that part go, and let my old wounds heal. Sculpting is like therapy because it is very calming and actually exciting when good things start to take shape. I literally feel blessed to have the ability to sit down any time that I desire and sculpt something that I know will make someone feel good. I am very thankful for my ability to do just that. Not only does it help someone else but it is enormously therapeutic to myself. I sculpt most everyday…guess I need a lot of therapy. It is actually also just fun to me. I have written and created some of very best work at my lowest moments and doing so helped bring me back to the surface.

Last Words

If I were to have the choice of my final words to you,

those would be to trust in God,

for He will get you through.

Though, I love you more than words can truly ever express,

His love is greater than even mine,

for He loves you the best.

When I am no longer around to spend time with you,

He is here forever and always, and for everything you do.

So I know you will find comfort in the power of His love.

You won't be lost without me here,

if you have faith in what's above.

What Would You Do if You Lived in a Zoo

What would you do if you lived in a zoo?
Would you swing from a branch in a tree?
Would you flitter and fly like a bird in the sky,
or swim like a seal in the sea?
Would you walk around with your head in the clouds,
or just sleep on a rock all the day?
Would you jump? Would you hop?
Would you flutter and flop?
Would your dinner be worms or be hay?
Would you run and play in the sun all the day
until you were absolutely ready to drop?
Would you hang out in trees and eat lots of leaves
until your tummy was ready to pop?
What a life you would have with your animal friends.
The adventures would go on and on.
Life in the zoo would be so fun for you
but I would feel so alone.
You would have no kisses and hugs,
just bananas and bugs
all the while you were there.
Oh, I'm so very glad that my own little kid
is not so completely covered with hair.
You walk on two feet, have a nose not a beak,
have no fin, scale or feather.
You are my love and my pride.
Your home is inside, not outside in all the weather.
Thus, you cannot live in a zoo because a bear is not you.
You are no seal, giraffe, or monkey.
You are my beloved little child.
You were not born in the wild,
so you best just stay here with me.

Career Plans

My daughter wants to be a garbage man,
a dancer, a lawyer, a bum,
an artist, a teacher, a singer, a writer,
a clothing designer,
or anything else that is fun.
She comes to me for guidance
but all I can give her is love.
She is so very little.
I'm stuck in the middle,
so I told her to be all the above.

My Girl

Dream big, little girl.
It's a great big world.
There's so much to do and see.
Chase your dreams.
Do wonderful things
but don't you forget about me.

There was always a couple of constants throughout all the ups and downs in my life. God was always there. He never bailed on me. I also had the comfort of a few little bundles of fur with paws. No matter what, God and things with paws always loved me which is hard because I am not always lovable.

Brown Eyes

Stop looking at me with those BIG brown eyes.
No, I can't take you home.
I've done that before,
and since then I have swore
that I'll live my life alone.
The last time that I tried this,
he got up and ran away.
But you are awful cute,
so what's a girl to do,
and you might decide to stay.
Okay — Alright — YOU WIN!
You made me weak in the knees.
Come on, man's best friend.
Let's try this again.
I just hope you don't have fleas.

What you are

Why is it that you get the best seat in the house?
Seems like I'm always running around.
I work, and I work, and work some more,
yet your feet rarely hit the ground.
It really must be nice to just have it all your way
but something must be done when there are bills to pay.
Don't get me wrong. I love you, and God made you what you are.
But if given a choice, I would certainly choose the life of a cat by far.

Wags

I've gained a few pounds.
I've lost some of my hair.
My muffins got too brown
 but dogs don't care.

My house needs to be mopped.
My fridge is pretty bare.
My dinner party flopped
 but dogs don't care.

My sense of style is lacking.
People sometimes stop to stare.
Someday, I may be back "In"
 but dogs don't care.

I may not be a hero,
so I'll just sit here in my chair,
accompanied by my furry friend
 'cause dogs don't care.

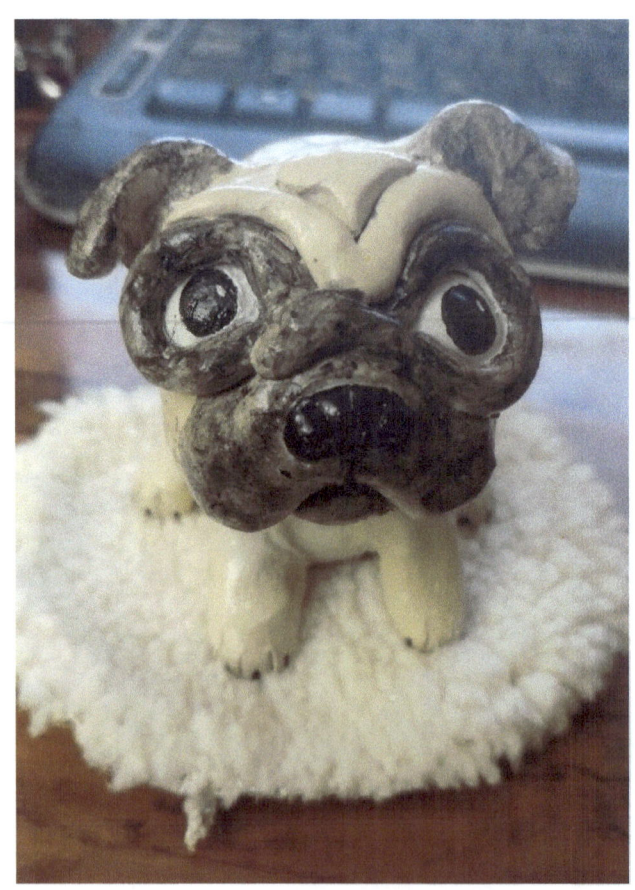

There will always be bad things that happen but I made a conscious decision to celebrate the good, the fun, and the happy. The reason why I sculpt in cartoonish style is because doing so preserves the good memories and makes folks (me included) happy. When I sit down to sculpt, things like this come out. If I am running low on happy, I sit down and just make it.

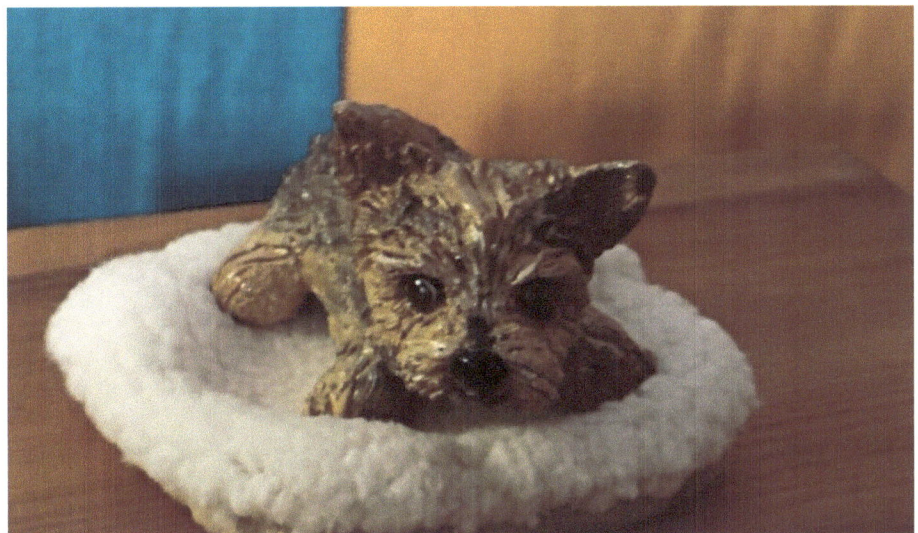

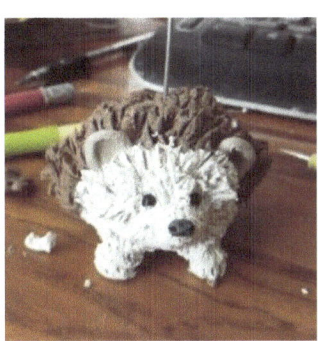

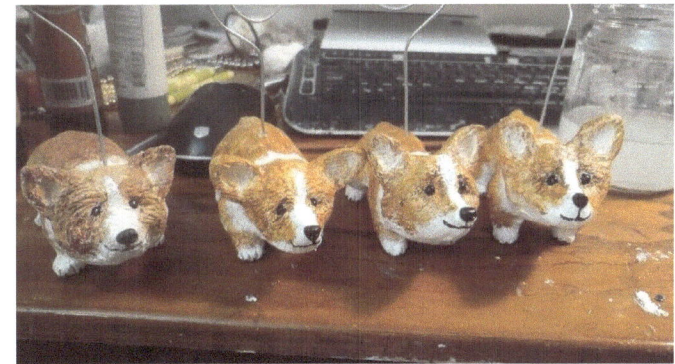

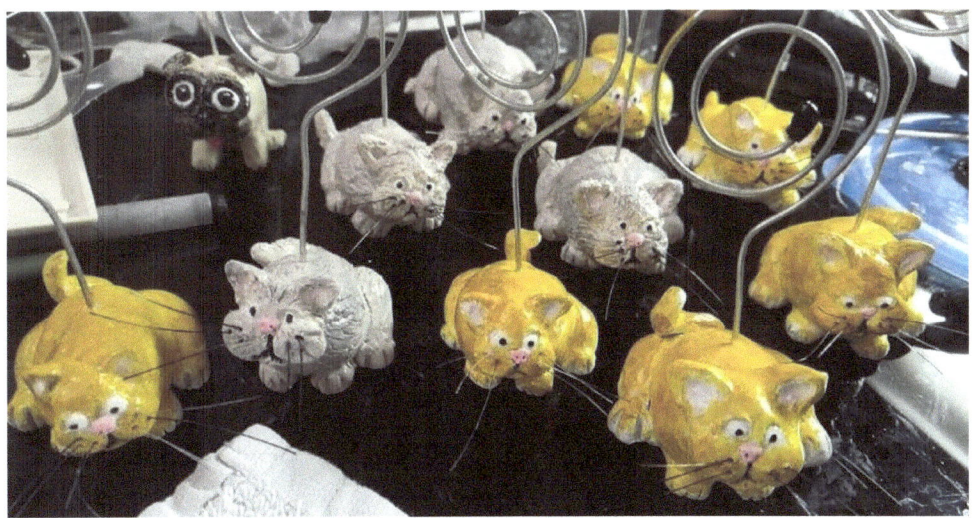

My alter ego Peg the Pug

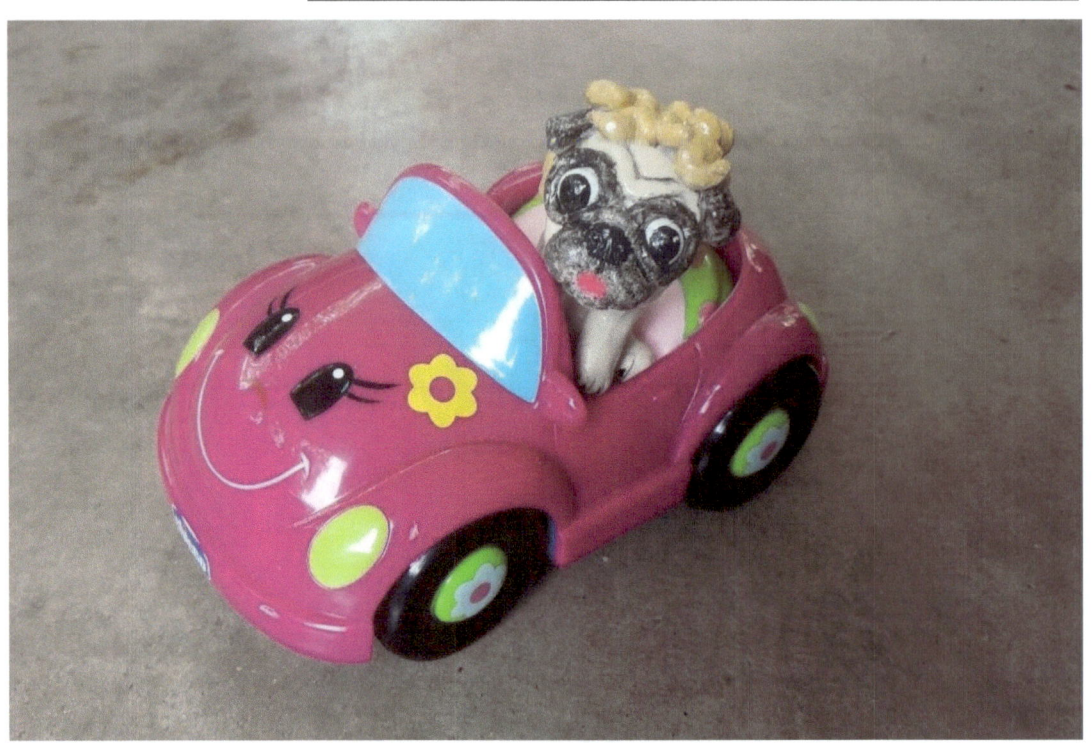

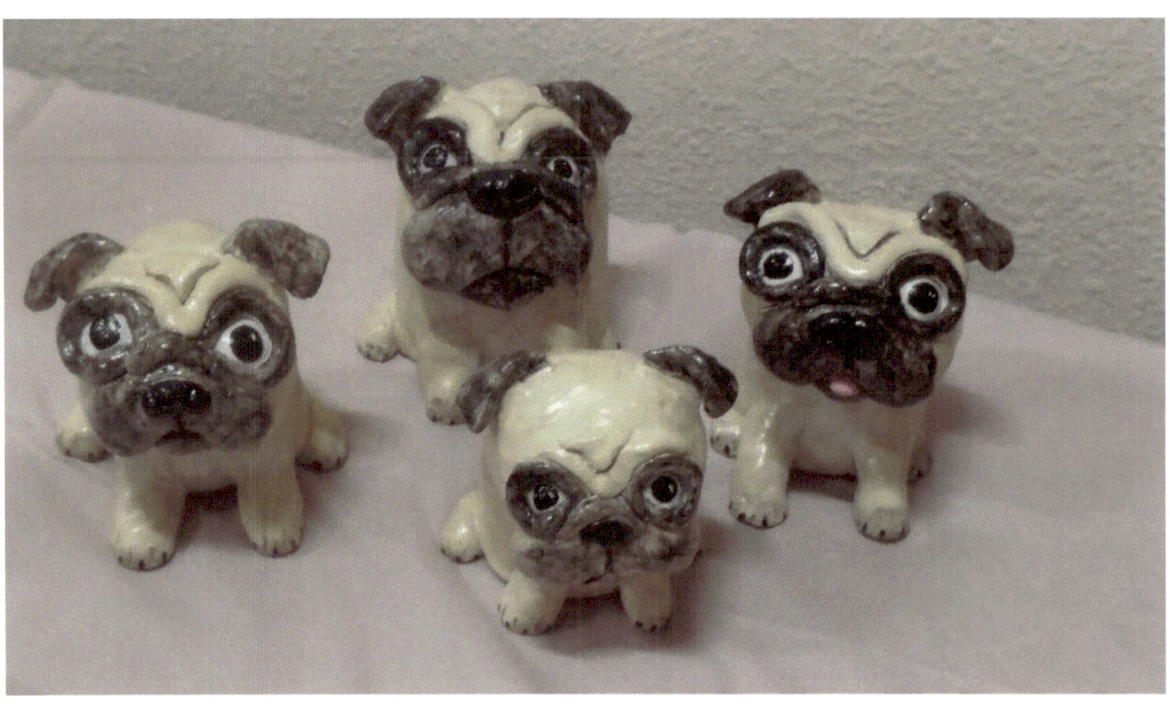

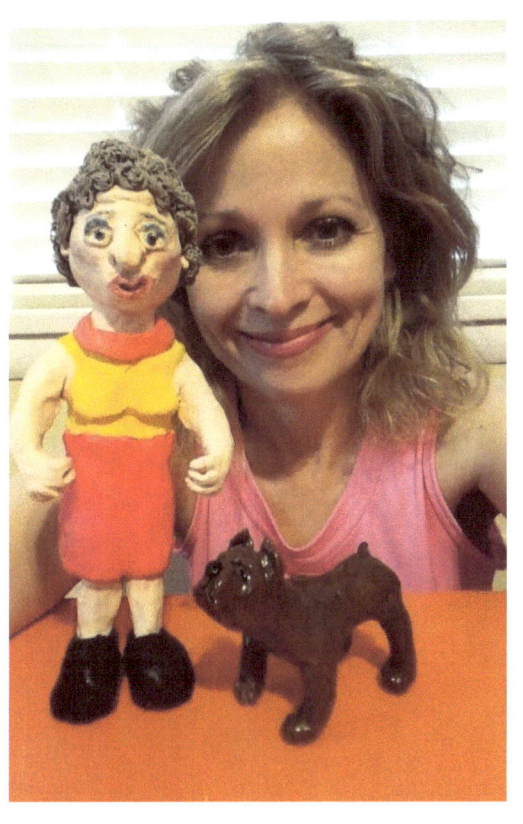
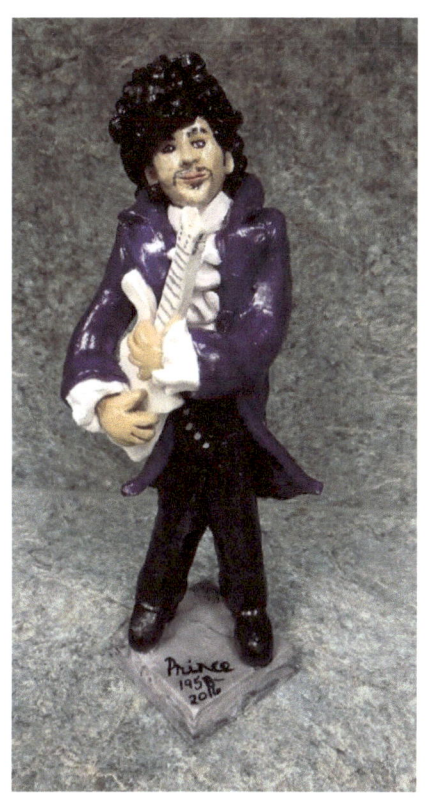

M.E.HUGS M.E.Best M.E.Thoughts
D. WELLS ASHLI D. WELLS D. WELLS

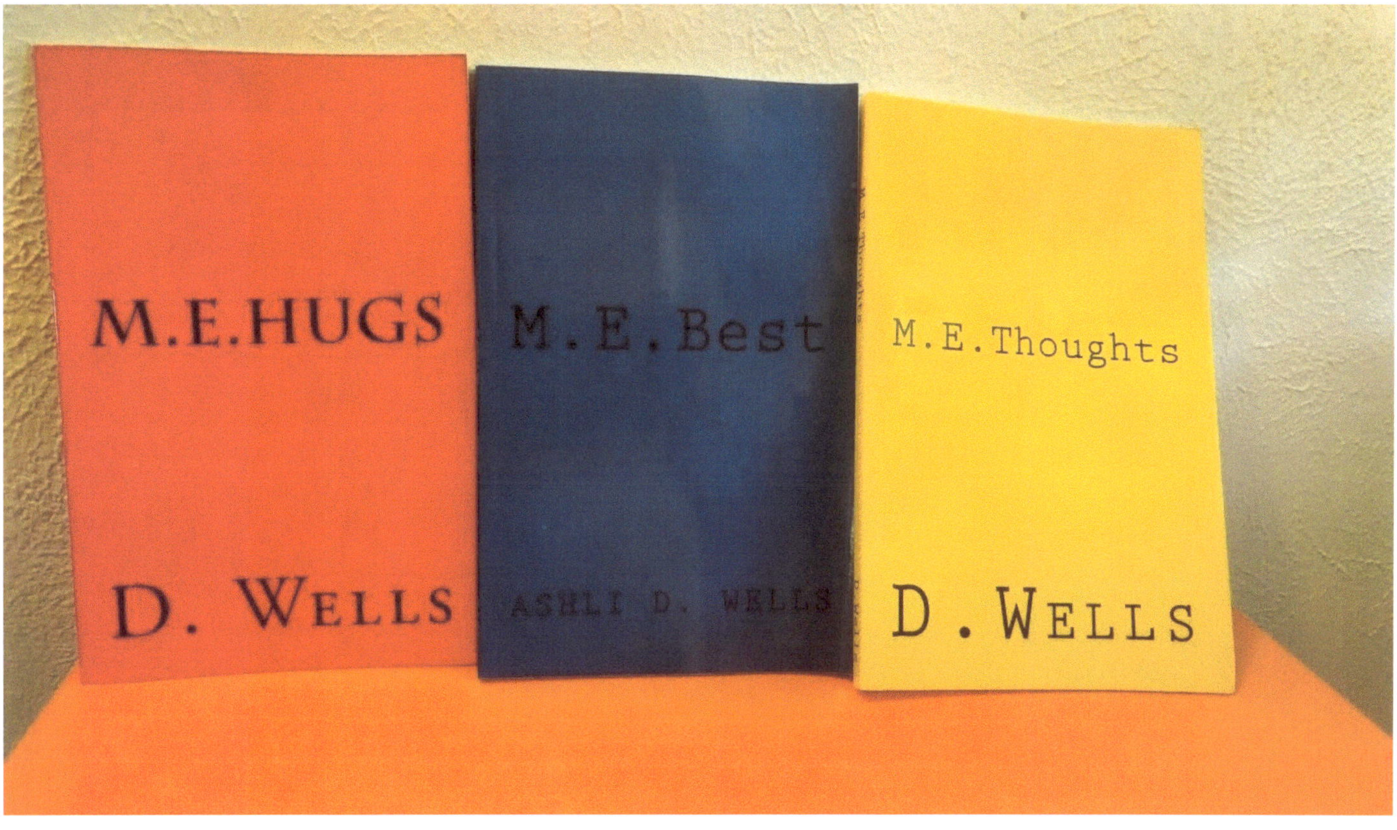

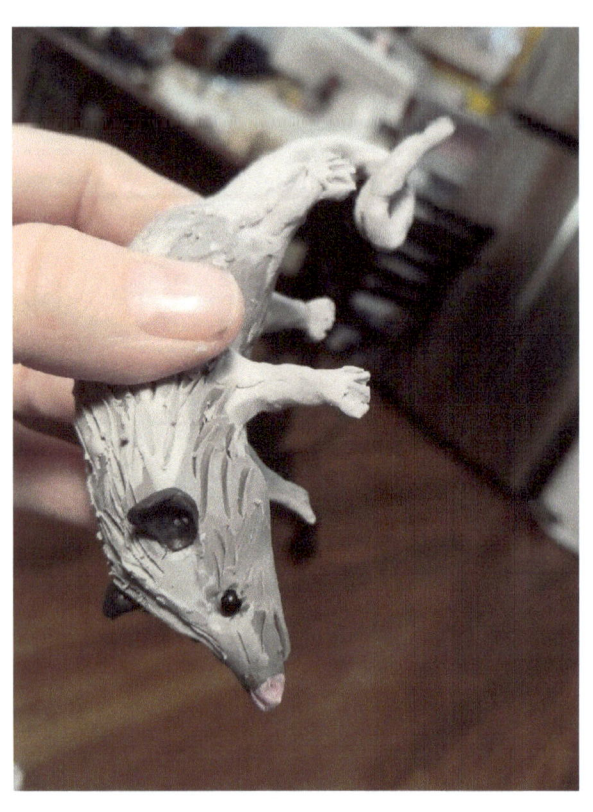
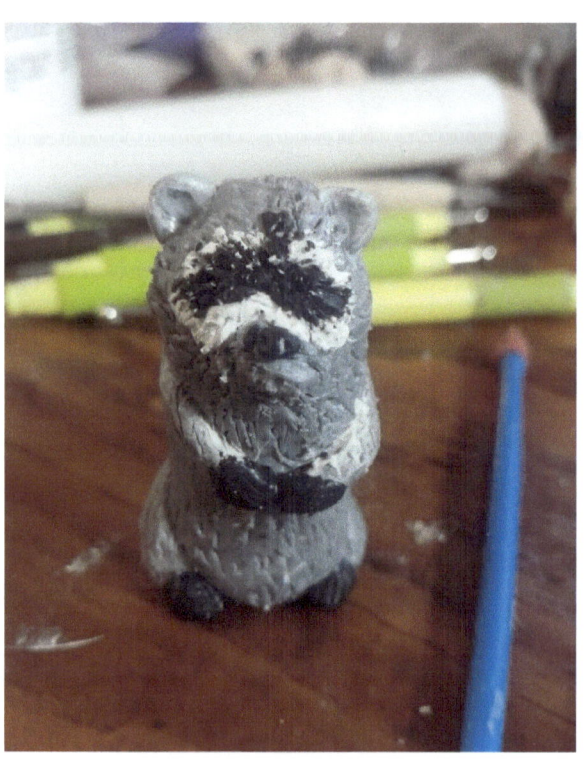
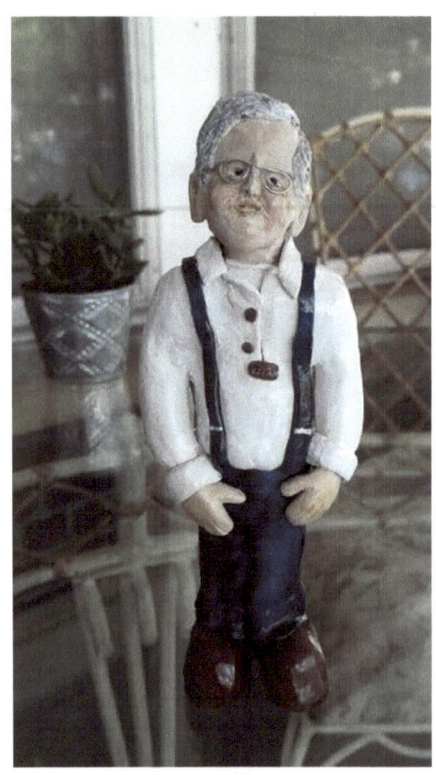
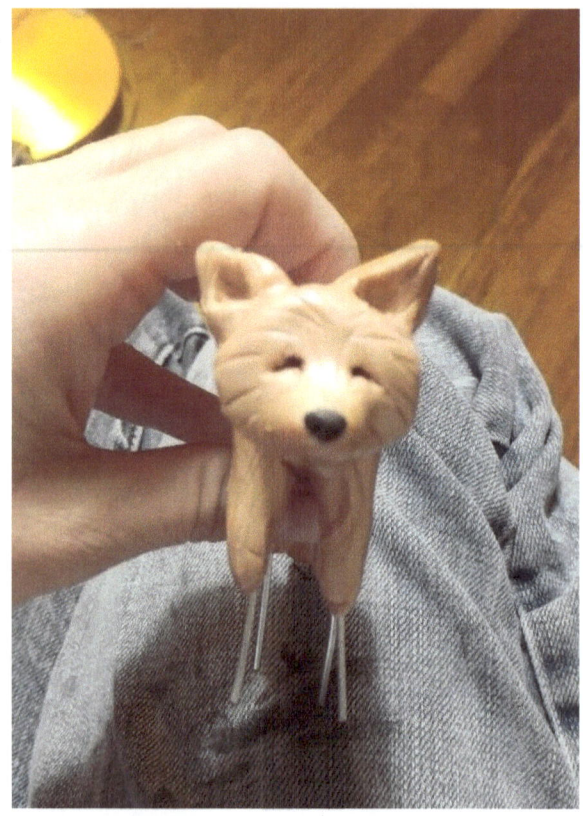

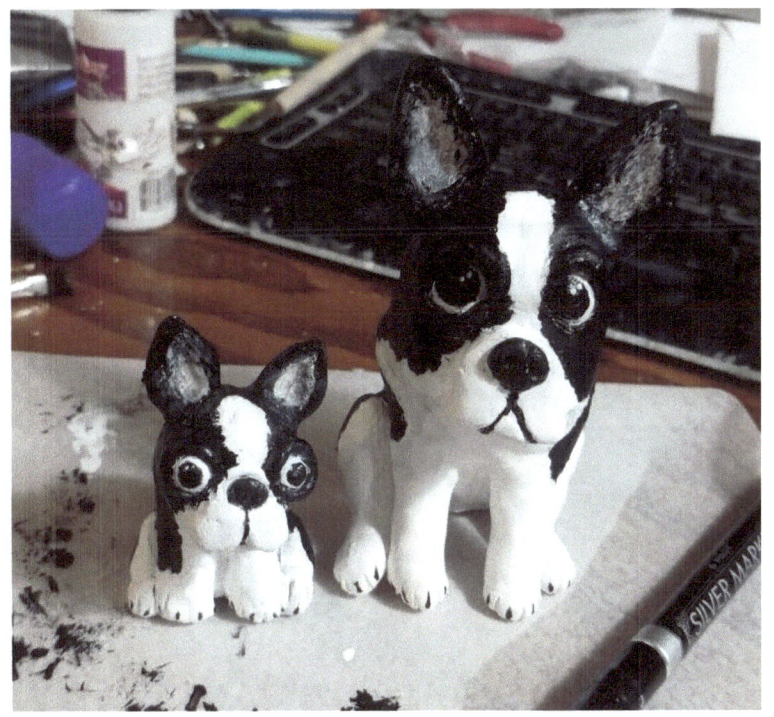

The Fort Worth Fur Department on Facebook

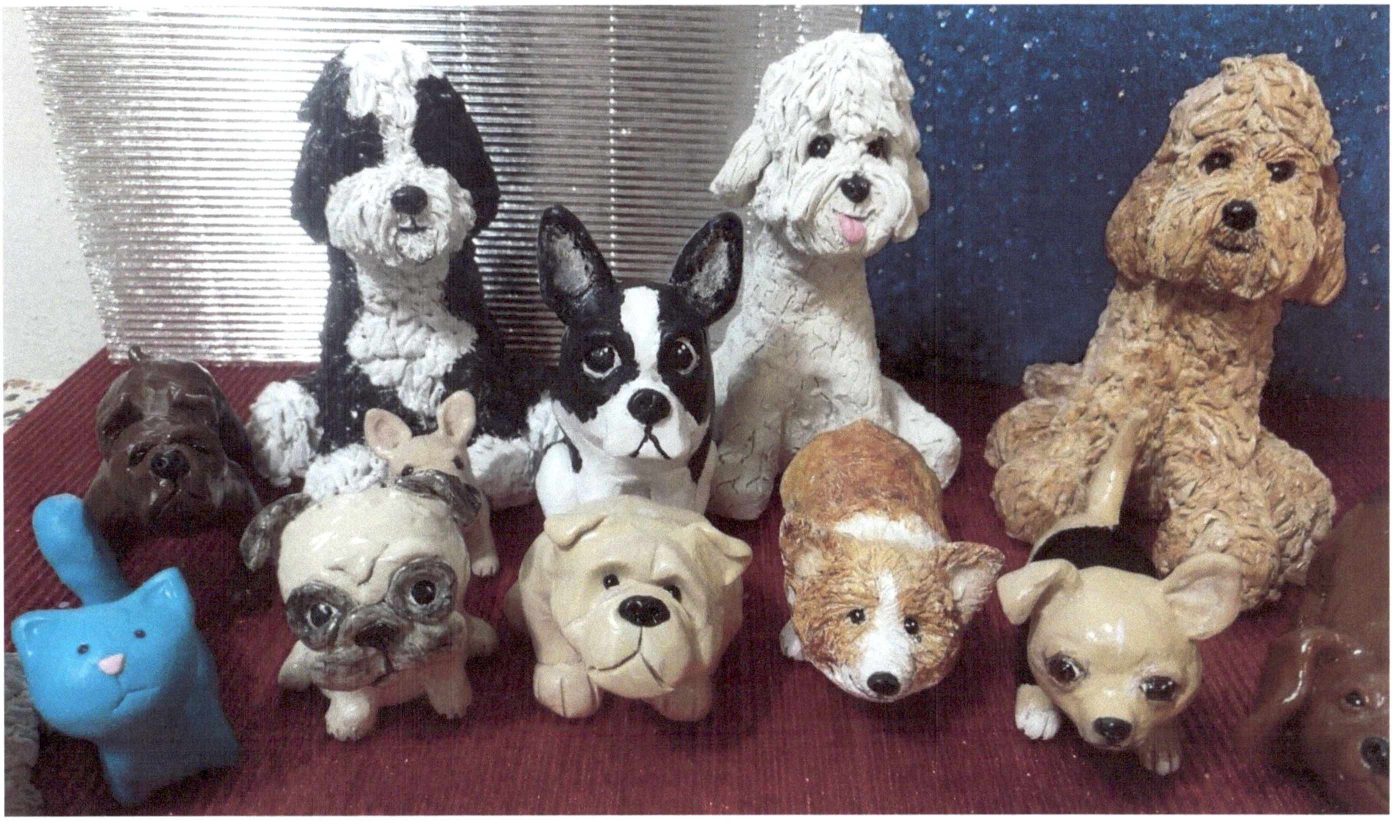

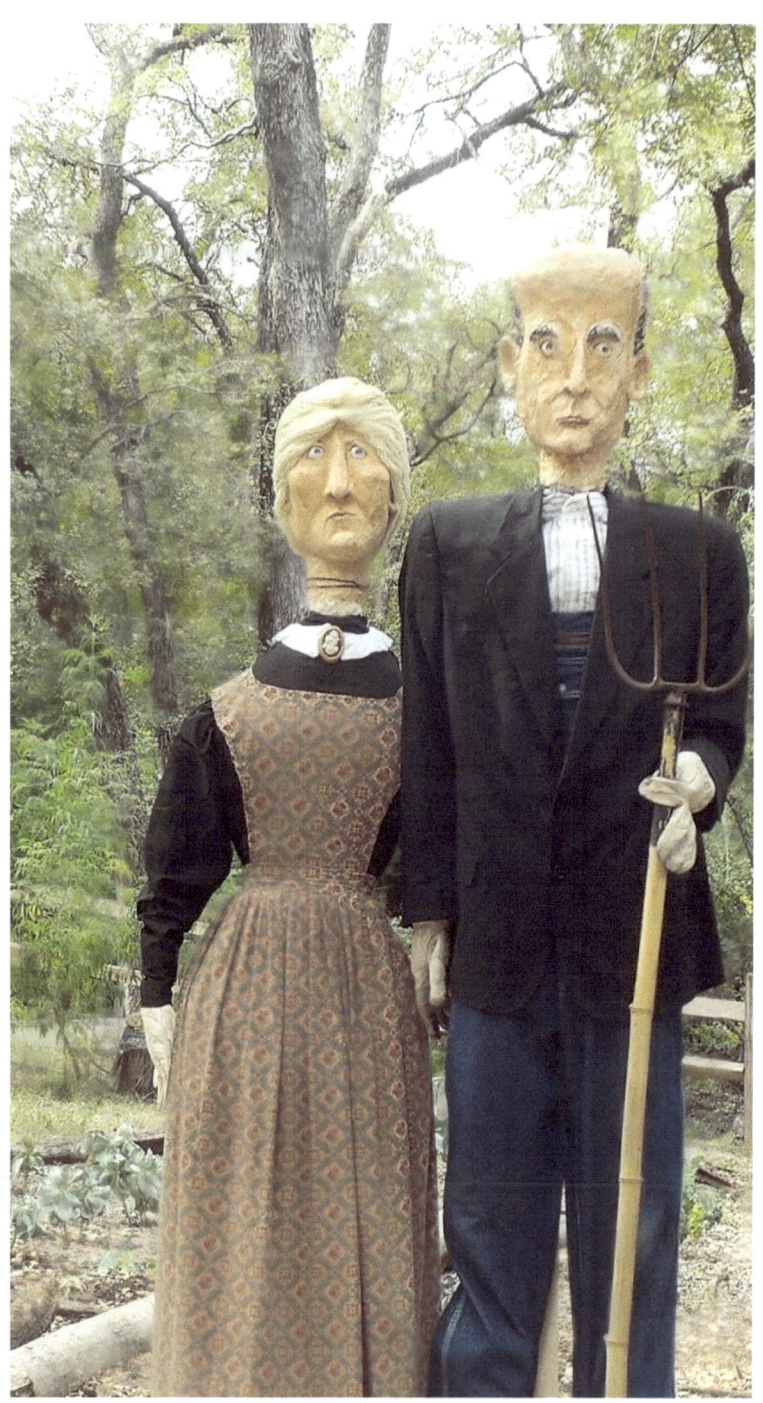
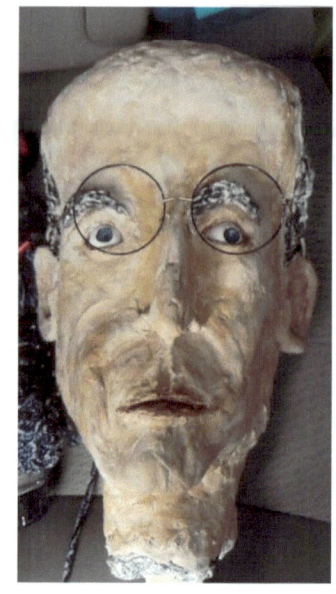
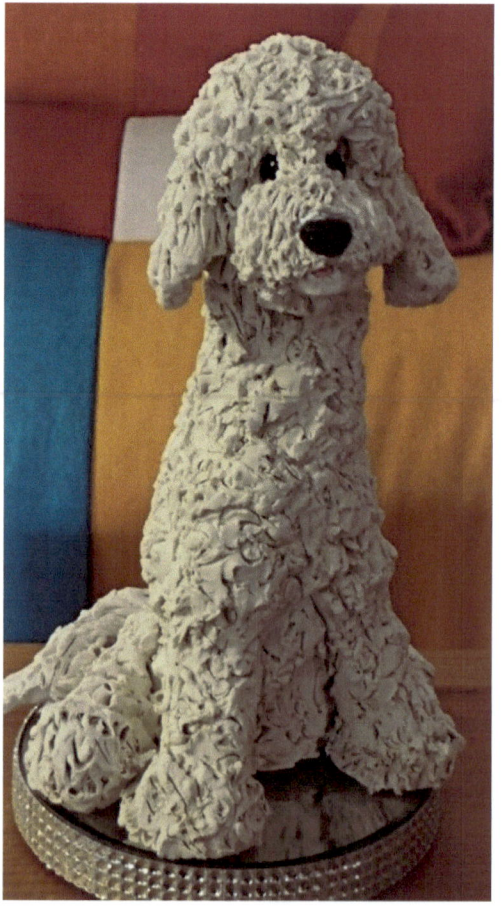

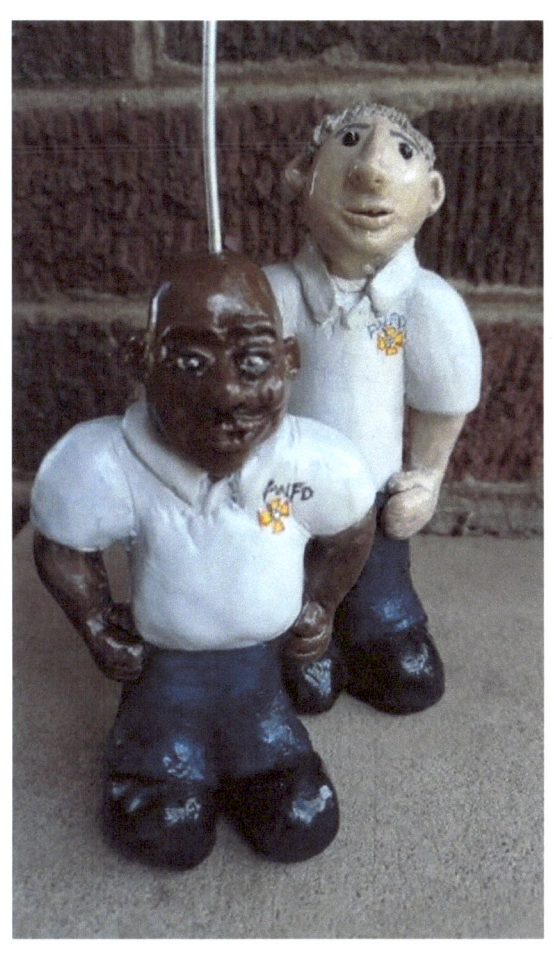
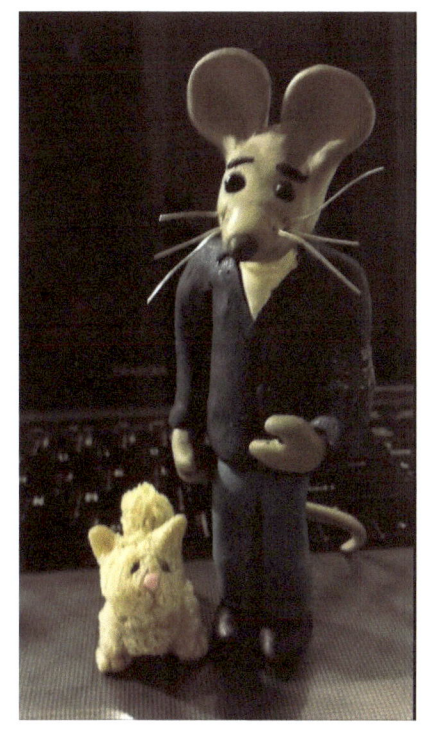
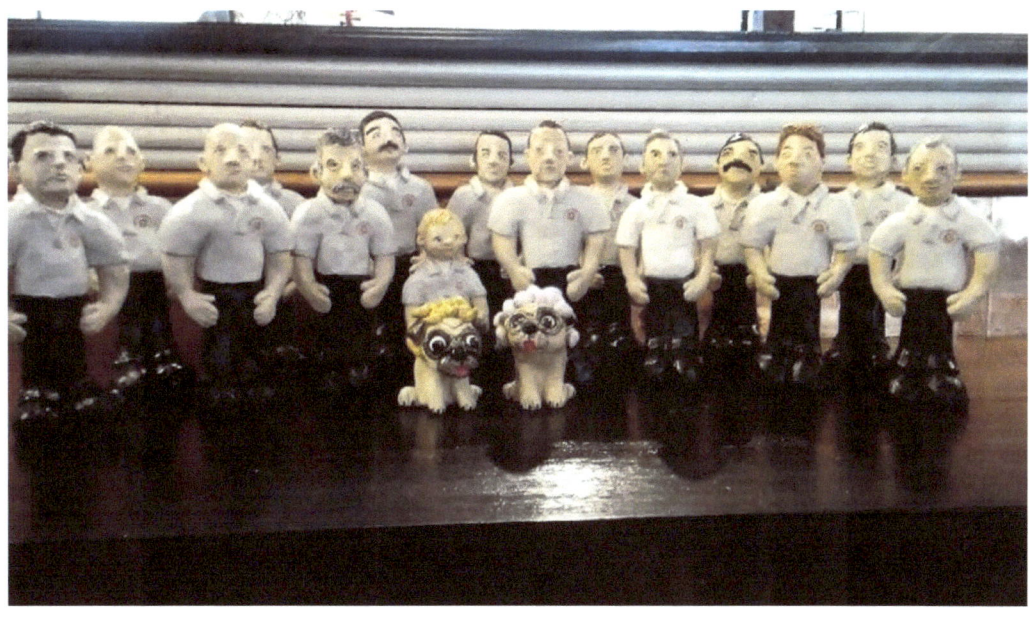

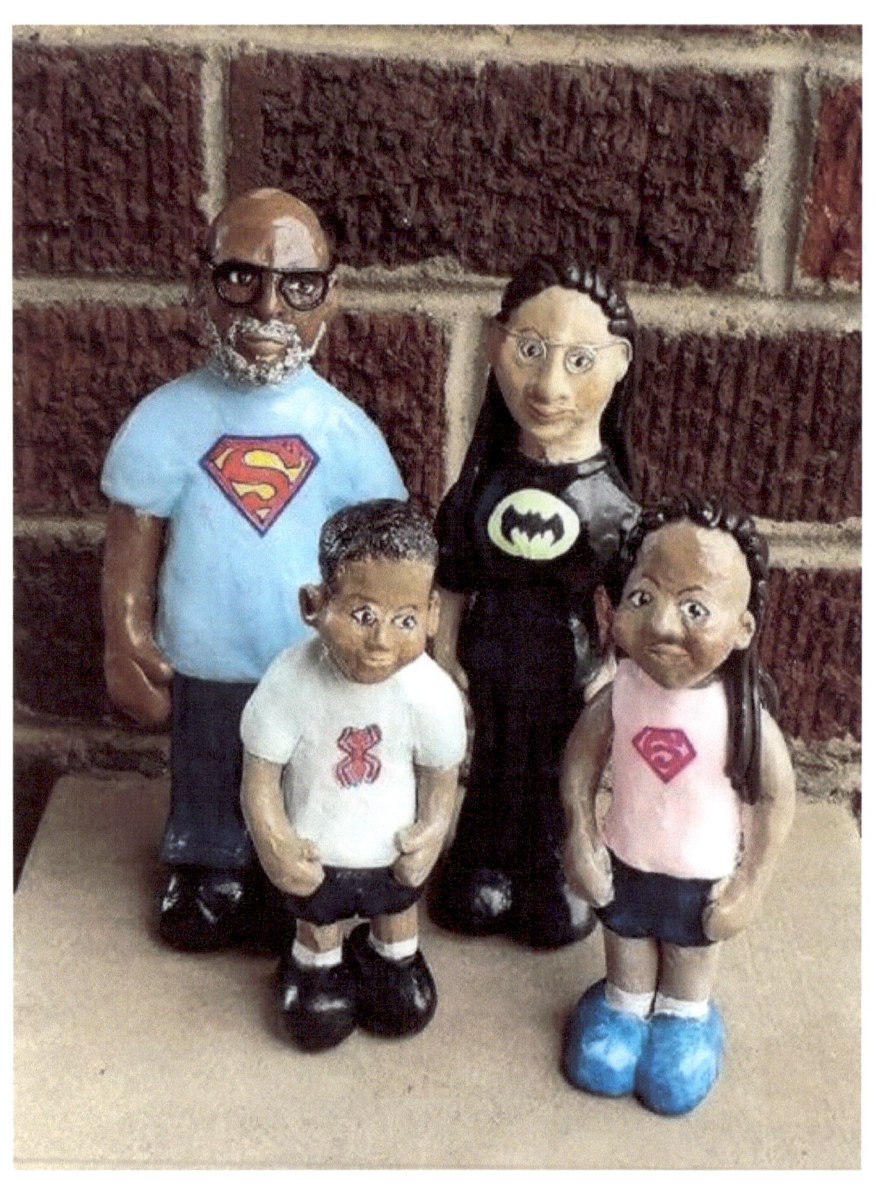
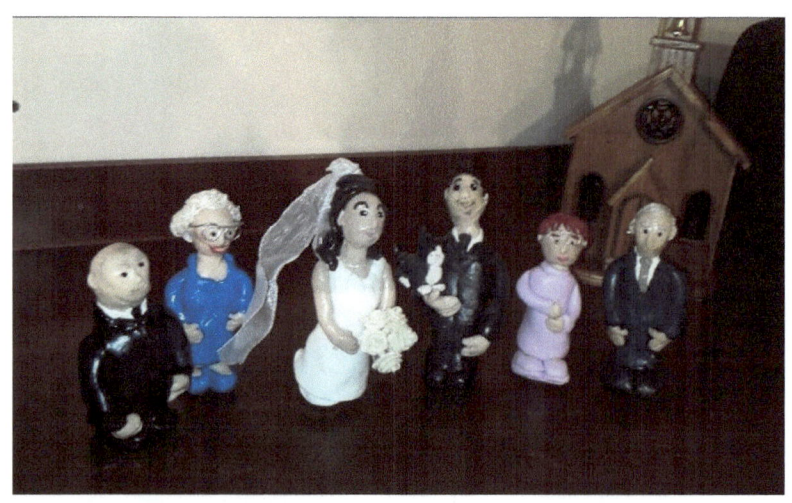

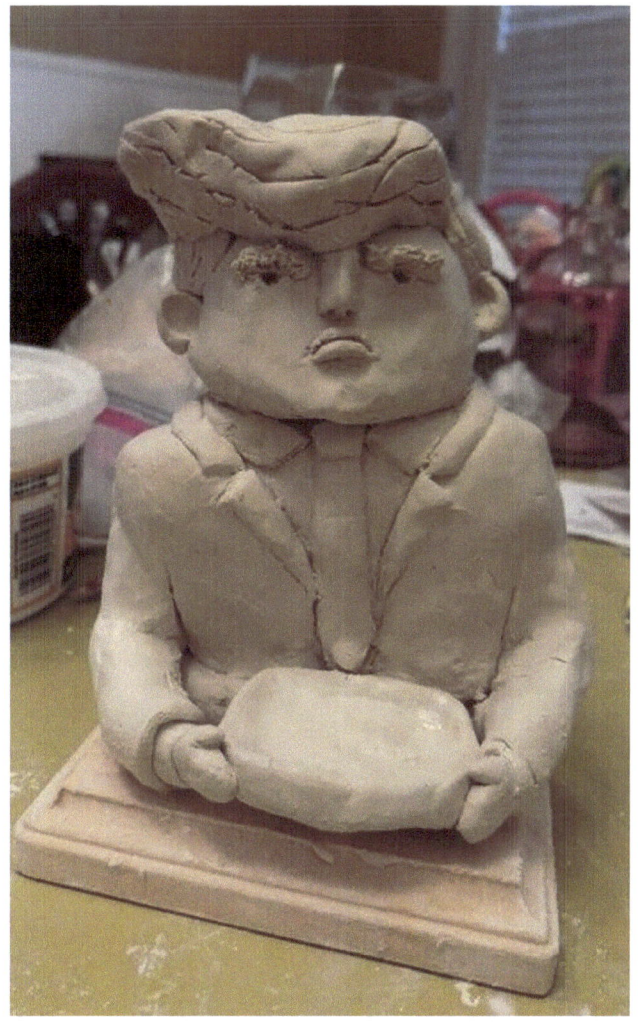

This is my only attempt at political satire. Lil' Donald was funny but I felt like a bully, so I destroyed him. I vowed never to make anything mean ever again.

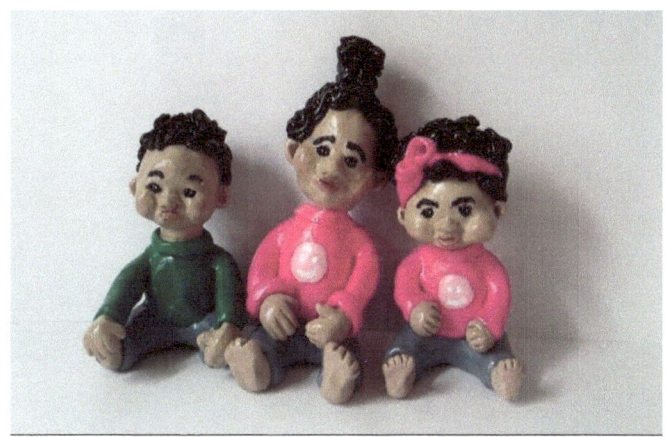

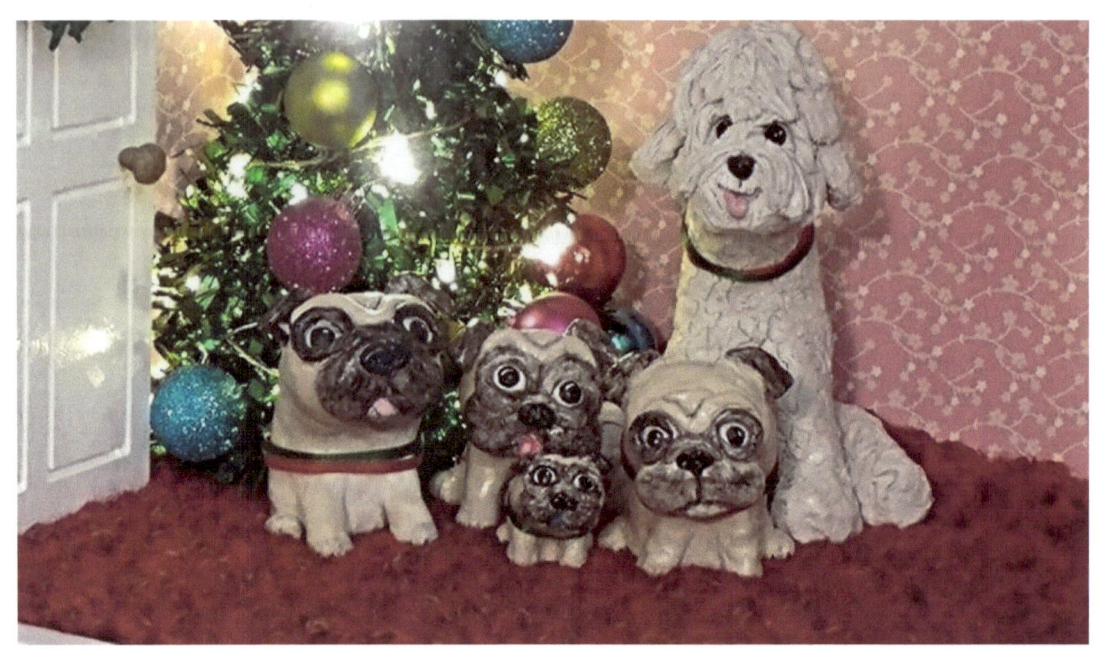
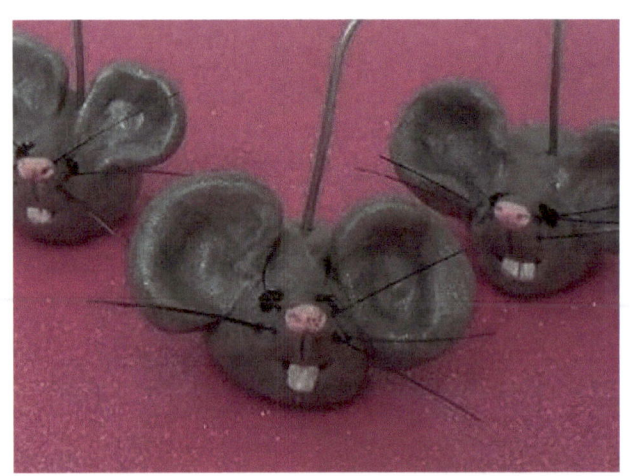
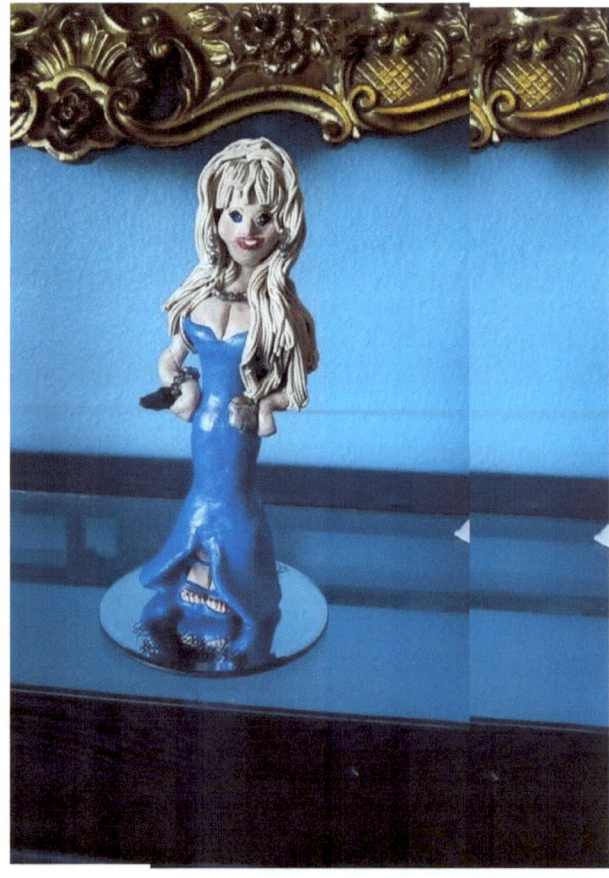

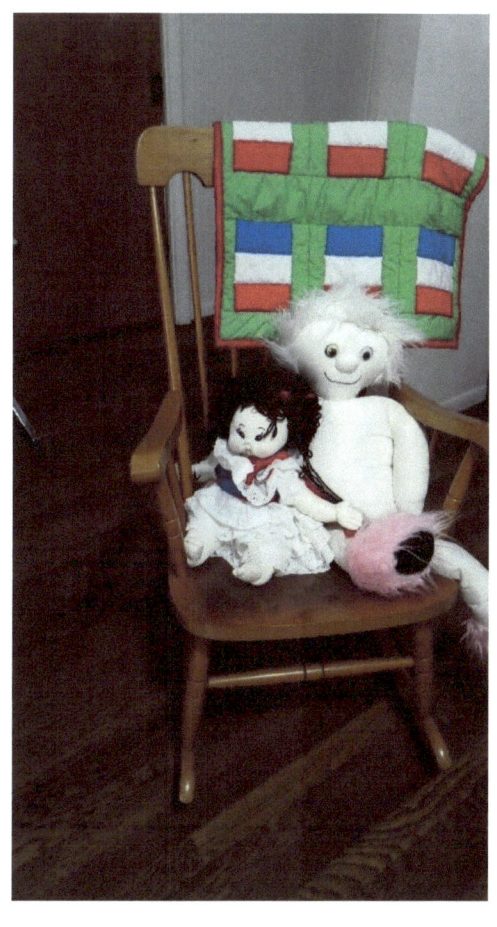
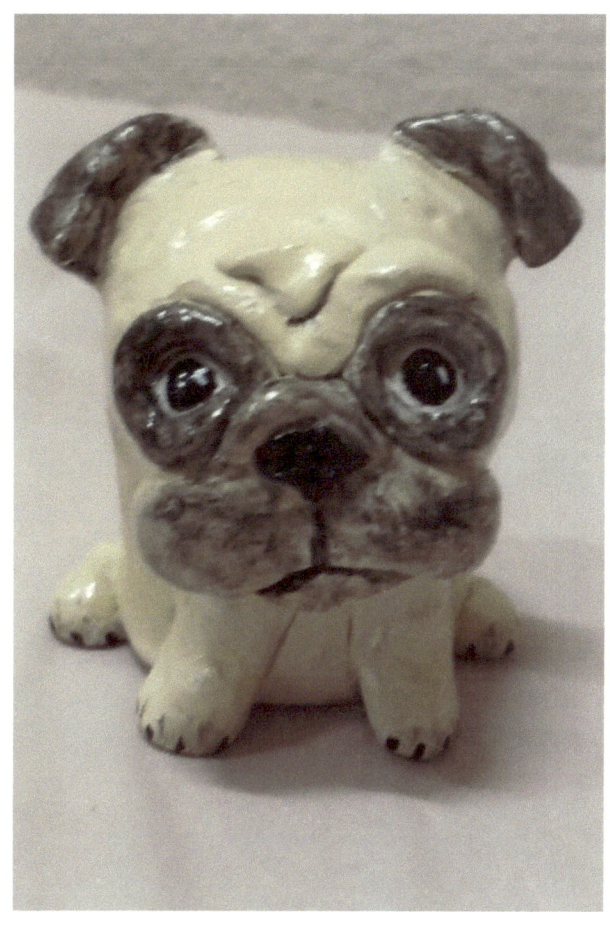
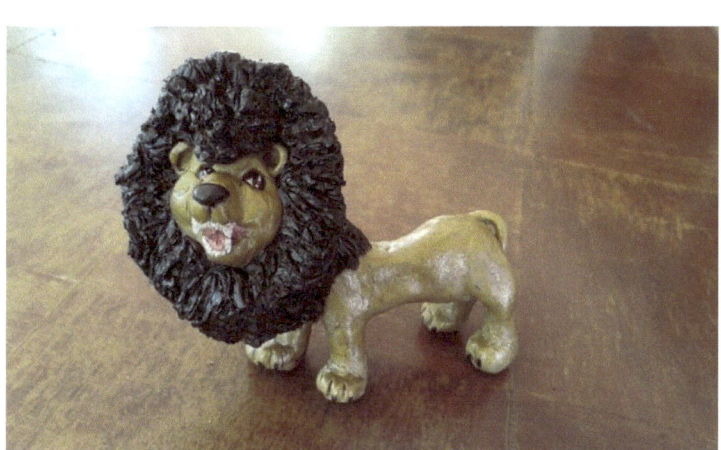
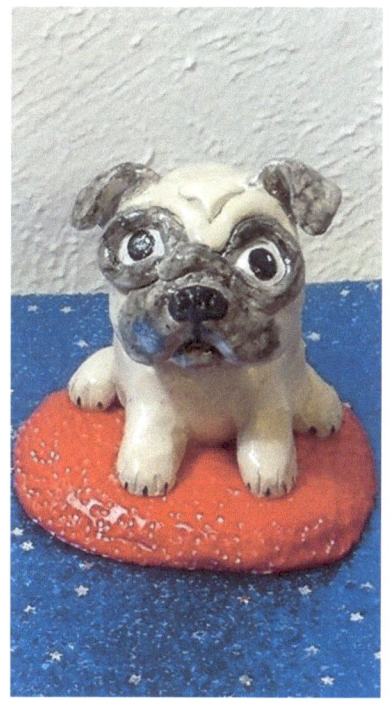

Pug on a Rug on Facebook

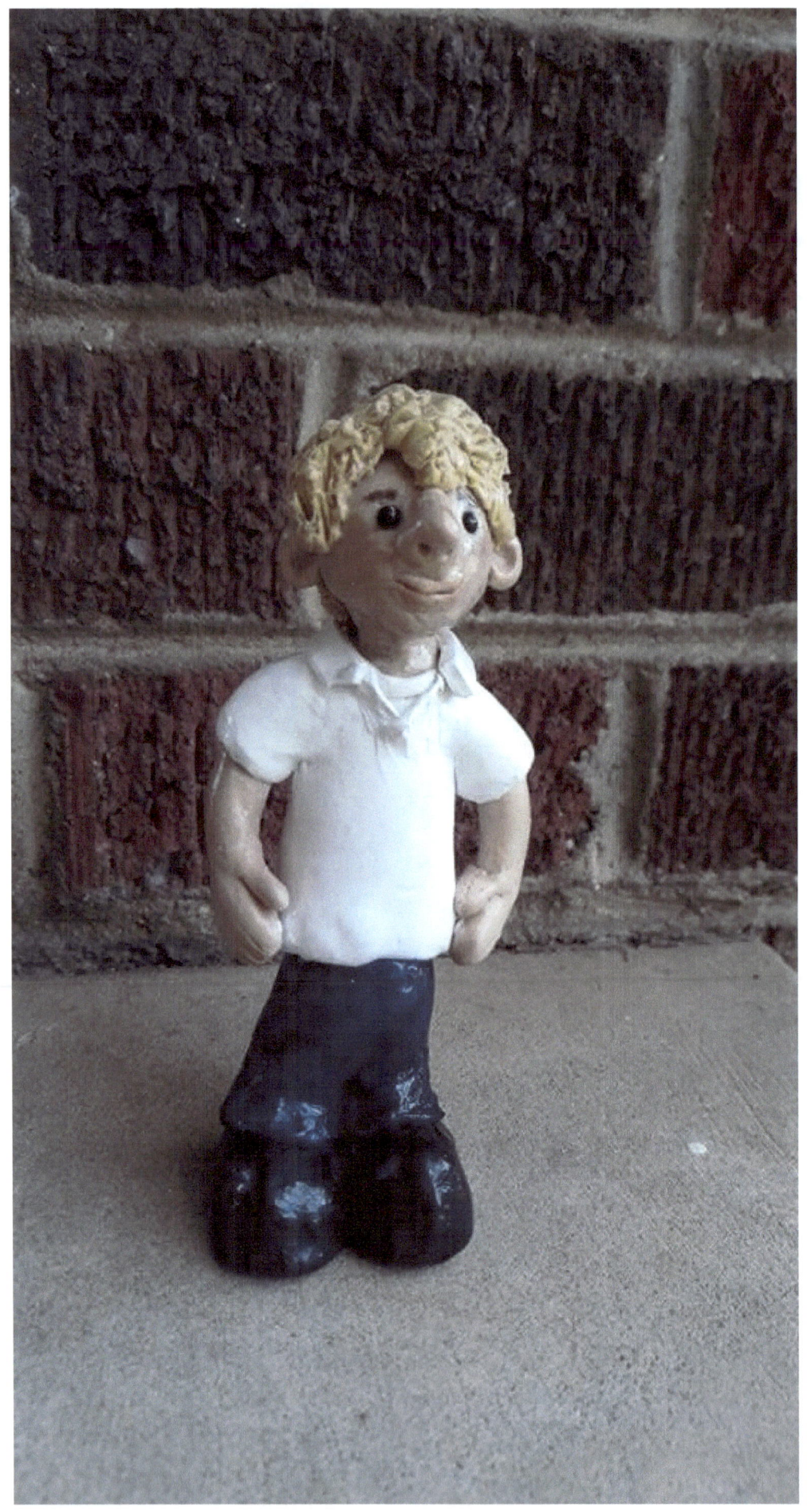

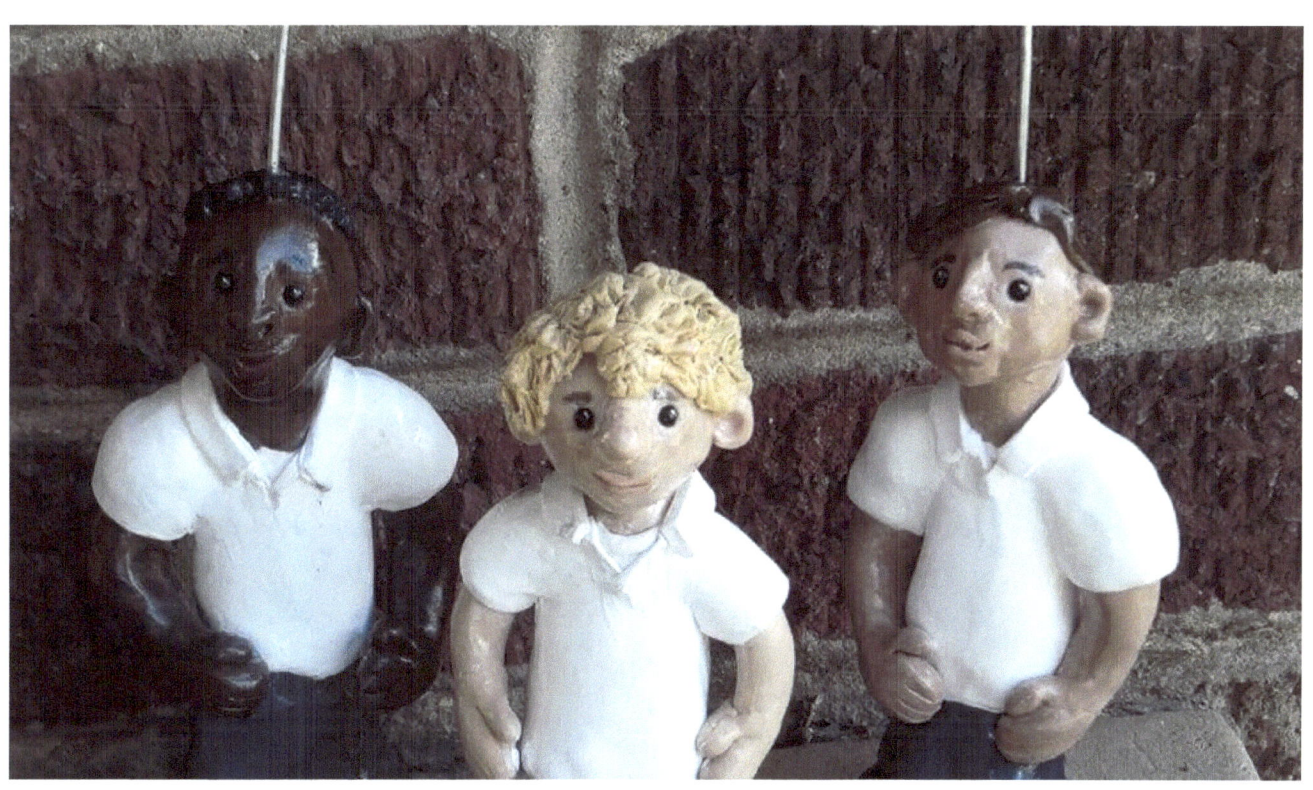

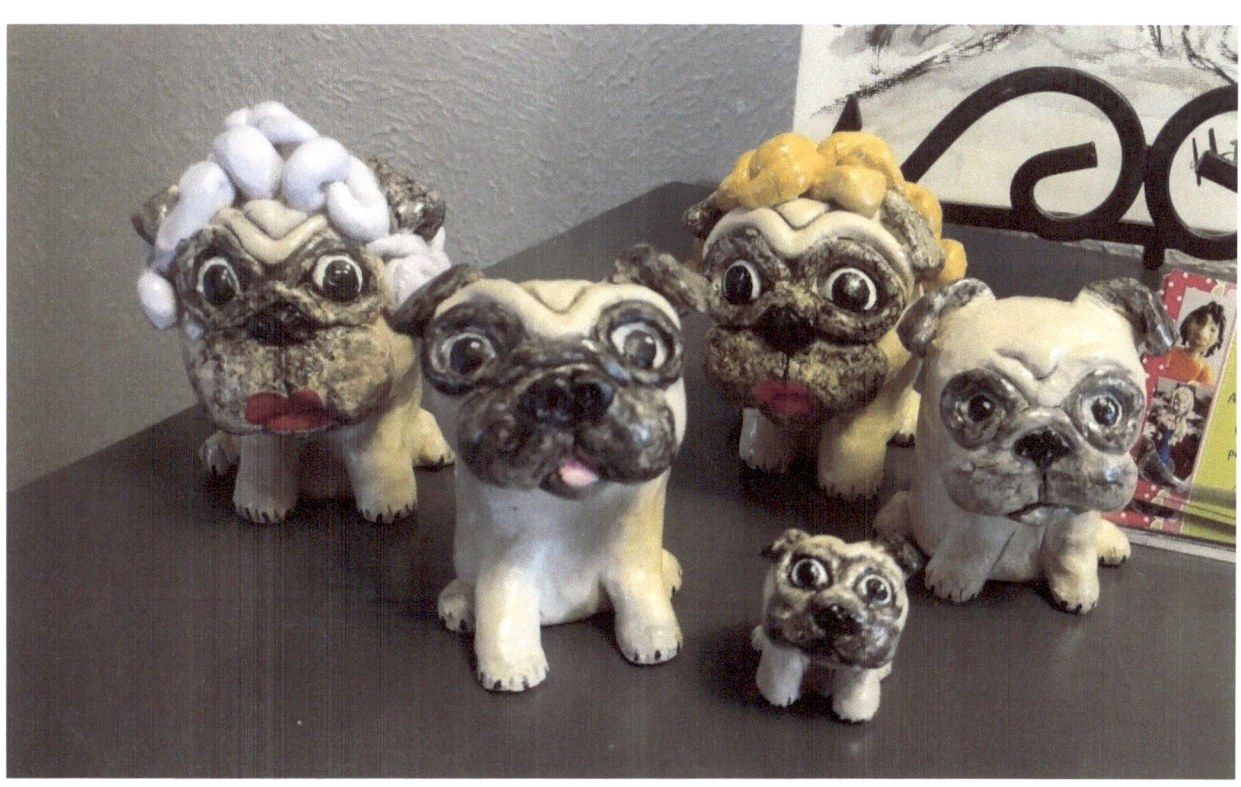

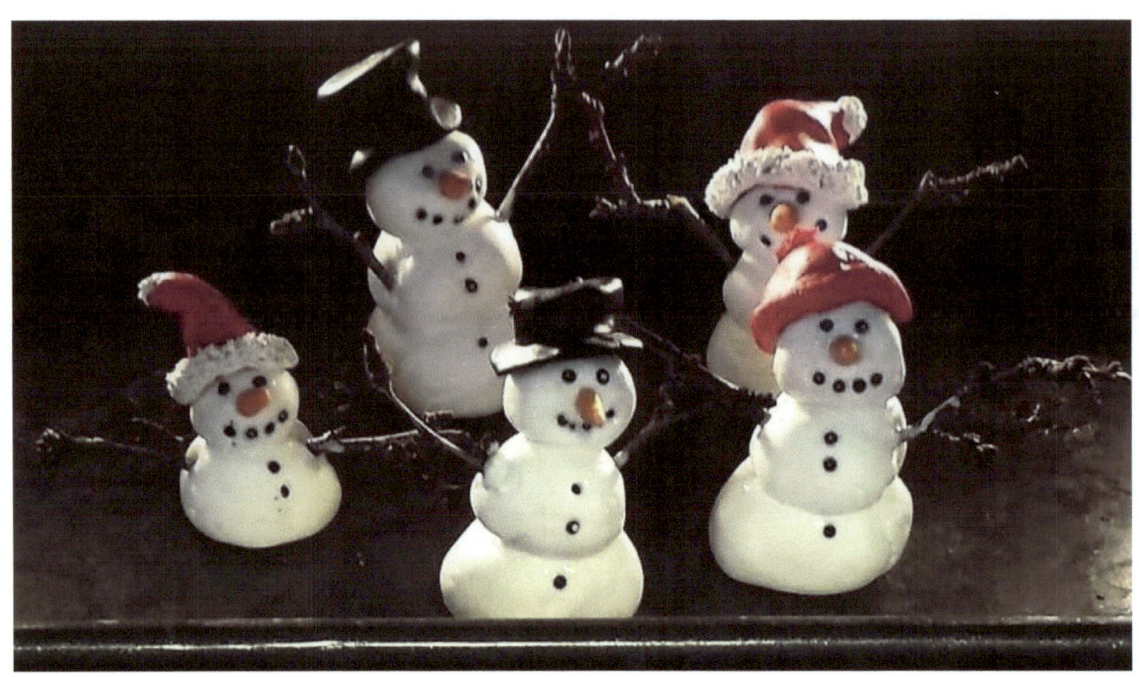
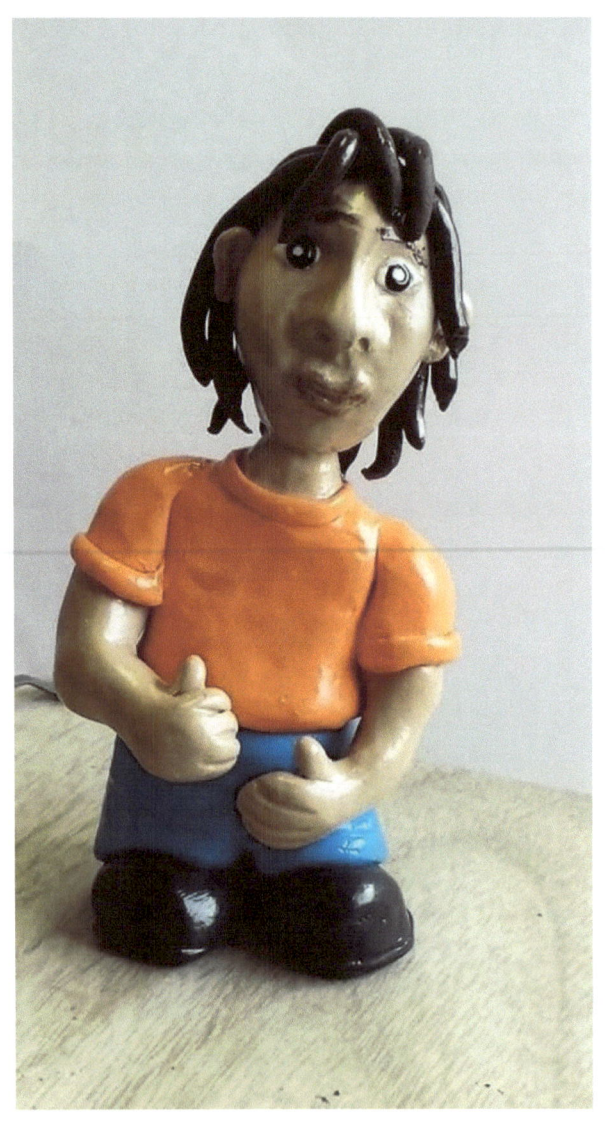
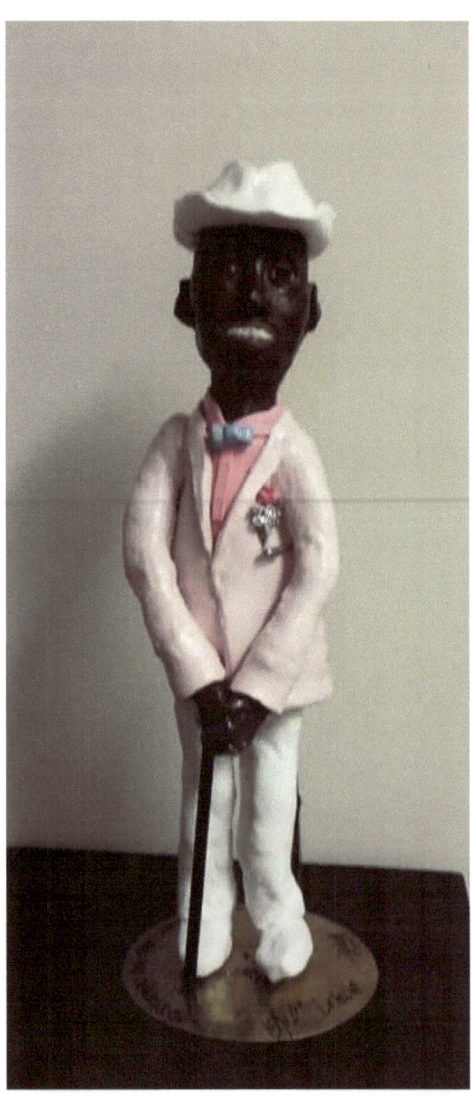

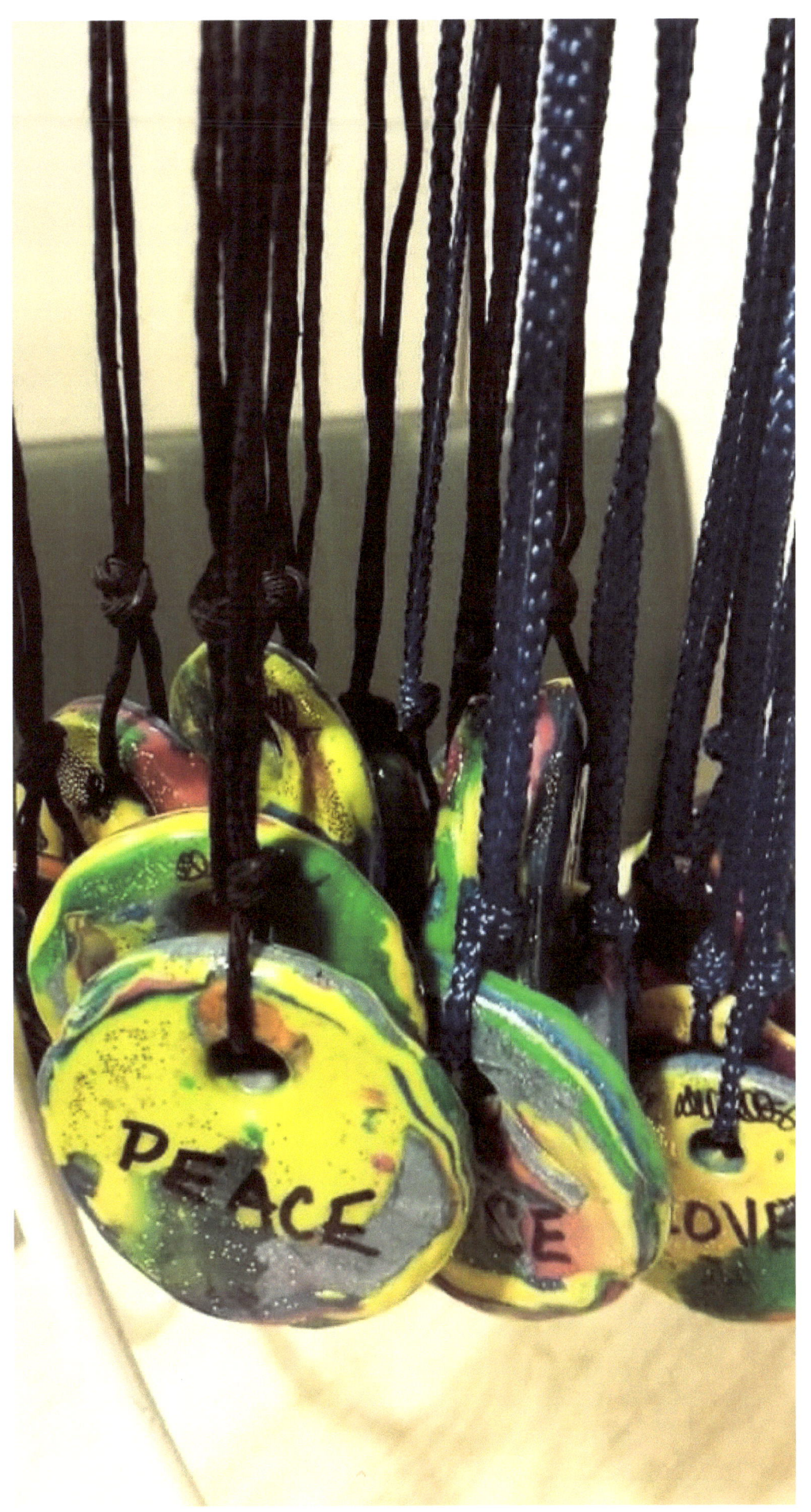

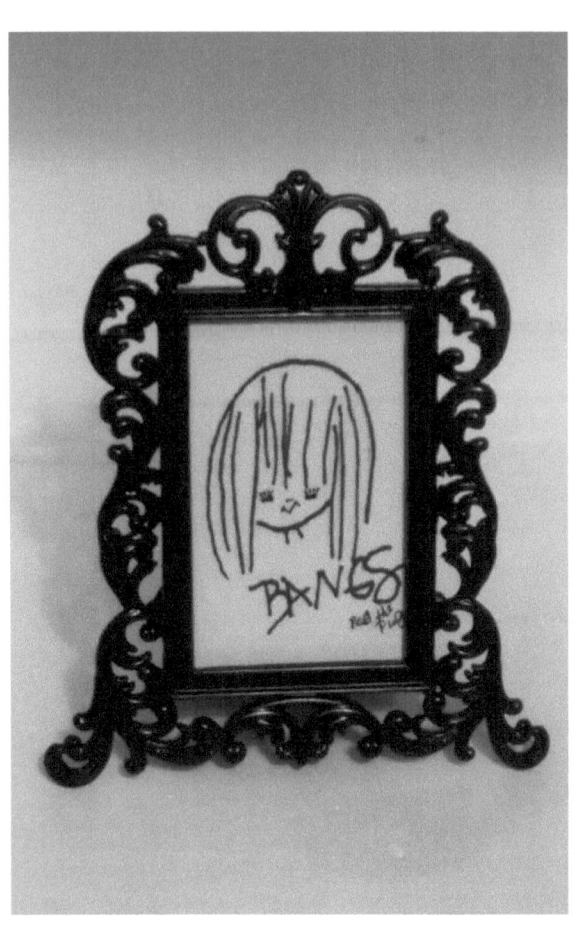
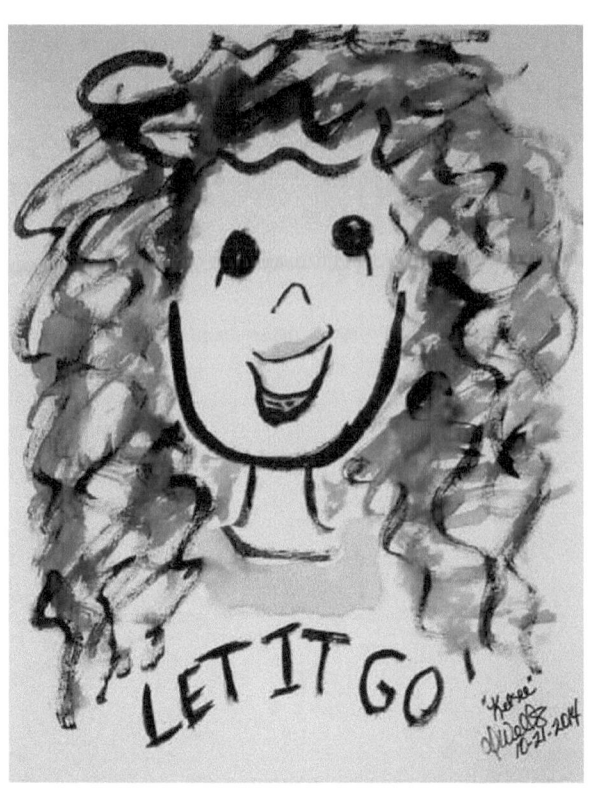
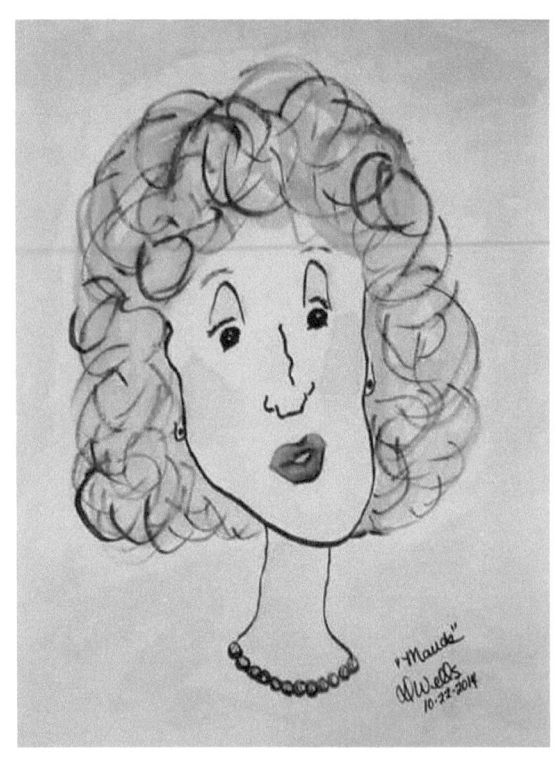
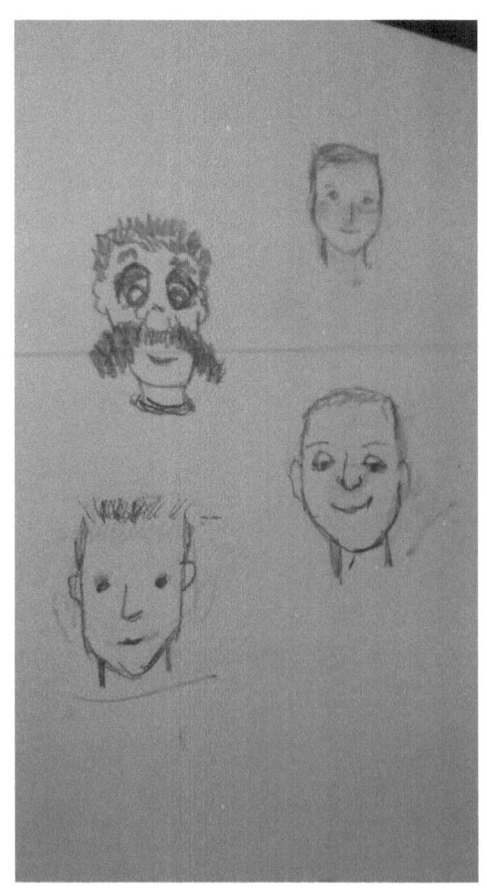

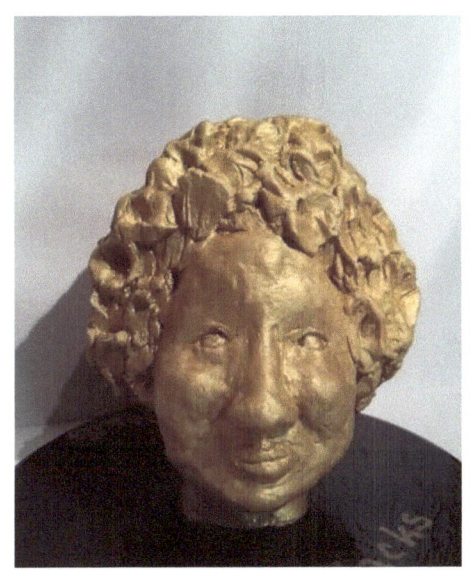
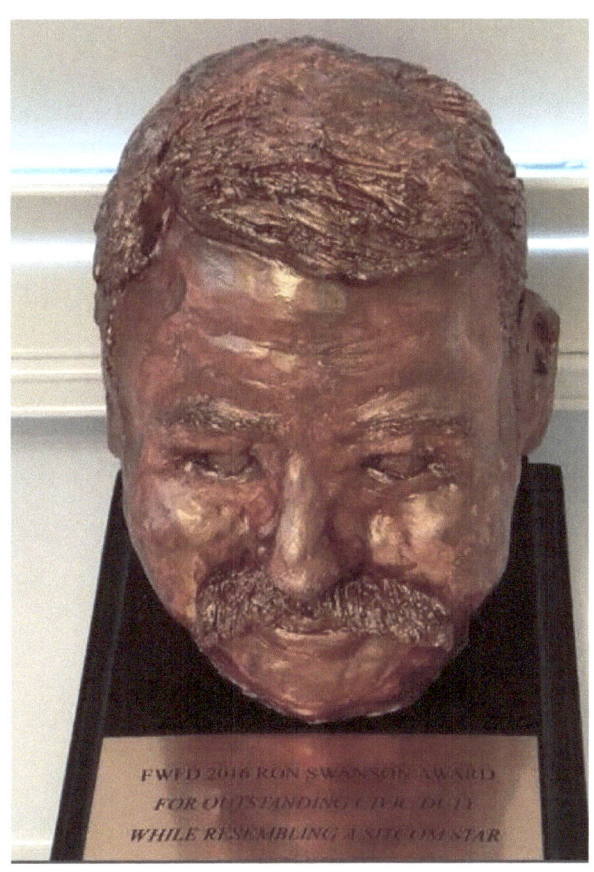

FWFD 2016 RON SWANSON AWARD
FOR OUTSTANDING CIVIC DUTY
WHILE RESEMBLING A SITCOM STAR

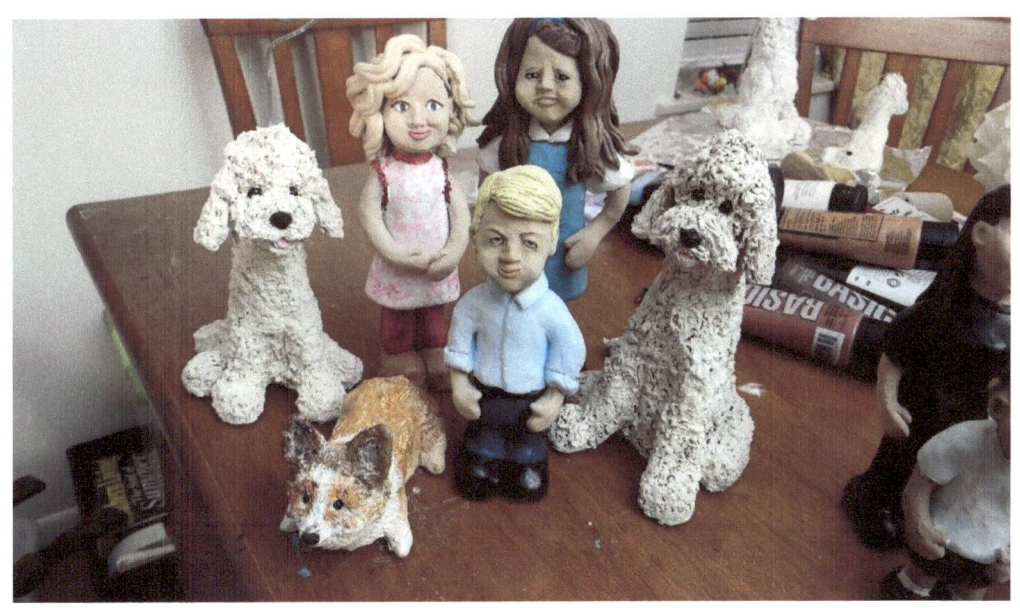

how I got started… I get a lot of folks asking me about how I got started sculpting. Truthfully, I have no clue. I have had a couple of brain surgeries in my life (no need for pity, pretty much okay), so I don't exactly remember why I first started to sculpt. I do know this is the first thing that I made. I sculpted these for my aunt and uncle. I do know why I started to write poetry though. I started doing that because at the time, I couldn't really physically do very much else. Anyway, sculpting and writing made me and other folks happy, so I stuck with it. I can't really tell someone how to make most of what I create because what comes out of me is the world according to me. The best advice that I can give someone is to not try to copy someone else. Whatever a person puts out into the world needs to be a chunk of his or her own self. However, to learn the process of sculpting, I read books, watched YouTube videos, joined art groups on Facebook. I also sculpted for hours and hours and hours over several years. Everything that I did to learn how to get started sculpting are things that I continue to do. I continue to sculpt hours, and hours and hours but I love to sculpt so that part is okay.

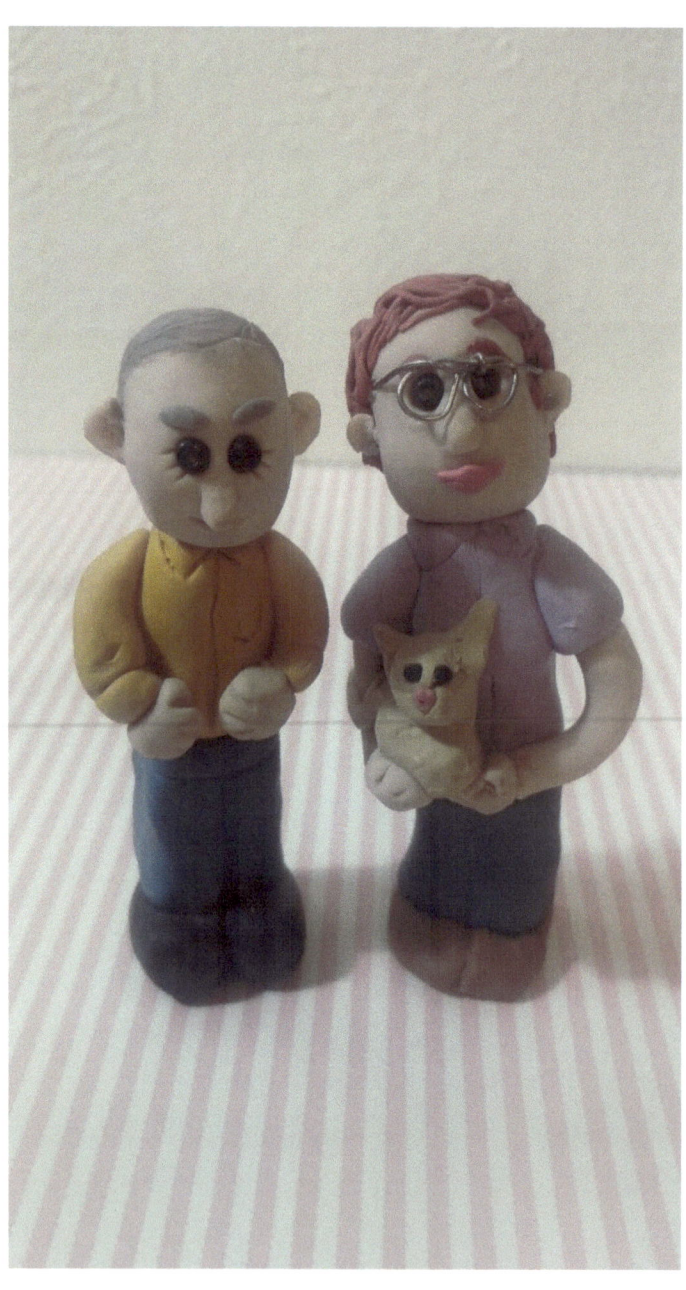

If you want to check out some of my other work then here is a list of my past, present, and future projects.

Completed Projects available on Amazon.com
M.E. Thoughts by D. Wells
M.E. Hugs by D. Wells
M.E. Best by Ashli D. Wells

Current and Ongoing Projects
Public servant sculpts
Pug on a Rug
The Village Peeps Characters
The Chicken Spies
Peg the Pug's World
Lil' A's Lil' Awfuls
The Fort Worth Fur Department

Completed Books Waiting on Illustrations
What Would You Do if you Lived in a Zoo
Todd and Shelly
Oh Taffy!
Rooster to the Rescue
The Village

Futures Goals and Projects
actually developing a workout routine
traveling to Ireland(do good to get to Target now)
loading all my art receipts on to my computer
developing Jorge the Hamster
having the thighs of my dreams
reading the entire Bible without skipping all the words I can't pronounce
being rich and famous(would settle for just less poor and unknown)
sculpting hours, and hours, and hours (which is okay because I love what I do)

If you need to contact me:
Facebook Ashli D. Wells
The Fort Worth Fur Department
Instagram ashlidwells

F. Y.I.

I don't tweet much and I am bad about checking my email, so use those means as a last resort to contact me. Also, I'm not really looking for a man, or a woman for that matter, so don't contact me if you think I'm your soulmate regardless of how awesome that you are. I can promise you that I am not the gal for you. However, feel free to contact me about anything to do with my sculpting or writing. Don't contact me trying to sell me stuff. I don't need anything. Don't send a friend's request to me on Facebook. I won't friend anyone that I do not personally know, and I don't friend most of the folks that I do know. I have about 15 Facebook friends on my personal account (most of which I have known for a few decades) and even that seems a little too many to me. I'm totally fine being an introvert and have no desire to change that. I keep a very small inner circle which is the way that I choose to do things.

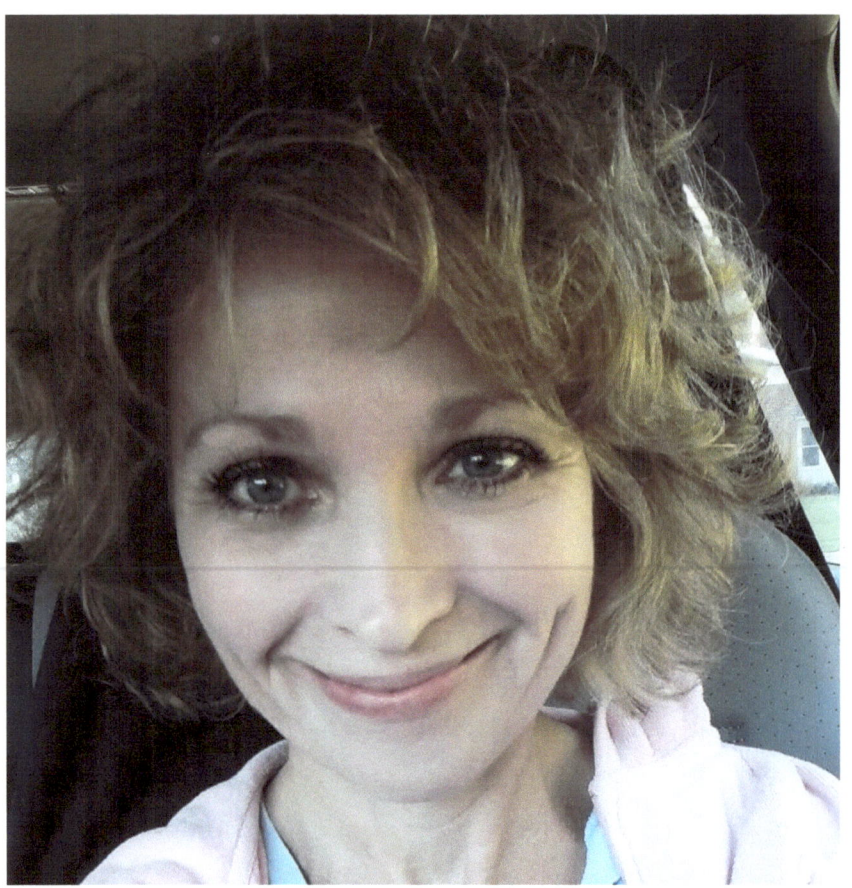

Thanks, Ashli D.

www.ingramcontent.com/pod-product-compliance
Lightning Source LLC
Chambersburg PA
CBHW051205220526
45473CB00003B/904